Manifesting on Purpose

A 3 Week Guide to Transforming Your Life
Through the Law of Attraction

Amanda Rose

ISBN: 9781983217890

attracts like). You can think of it as your Higher Power, God/Goddess, Energy, or whatever makes sense to you; for our purposes I'll be referring throughout this book to the power of the Law of Attraction as The Universe.

Now with this reflective power, the kicker comes in the way we think:

The Universe delivers; even when we don't want it to!

One of the most important things we have to learn about the Law of Attraction is that it is *always* at play. It doesn't take a break, so in embarking on this journey to set it into motion to create the reality you've always desired, it's going to take some work to start reworking our thoughts. Complaining about all the bills that just came in? Universe says "I hear you loud and clear, I'll send you more stuff to complain about! Order up!" Thinking about how you never have enough time, and you're way too busy? Universe says, "Great! I'll keep sending you tons of stuff to do!"

Now you're thinking "Whoa, but I'm thinking that I DON'T want more things to do!" Well, the Universe doesn't take what you do or don't want into account, it just delivers more of what you're thinking about. This is where the magic happens! You now know that all you need to do is focus on the things you DO want. Don't want all the debt? Start thinking "I am debt free!" Don't want to be so overwhelmed? Start thinking "I have lots of free time to enjoy my life!"

The Law of Attraction teaches us we need to be grateful for what we want *before* we receive it. In the coming weeks we will be going over exactly how to do that! To bring you more joy, happiness, wealth, health, love, improve your relationships, and start building your Dream Life!

But before that we need to dive deep into your mind to uproot our biggest saboteur:

Your Subconscious Mind

Thoughts are habitual, like the majority of what we do in life; after all, if we had to give serious thought to mundane tasks like washing dishes, or getting dressed in the morning, we'd have to be very focused at all times just to make it through the day! Instead our brain knows these things from routine and therefore we can effortlessly glide through these tasks. On the flip side, we don't question or shake up our habits often; including the way we think.

These thoughts are governed by our subconscious mind, which is why until we change that then ain't nothing gonna change! If we think of our brain as a computer, then your subconscious is the hardware, and your conscious mind is the software. It doesn't matter how much software you add in or swap out, it won't fundamentally change the computer unless you reprogram or replace the hardware. So, we first need to figure out how we're programed.

As children our subconscious has no filter, it takes everything in and interprets it in simplest terms. This is how we learn to survive, and identify the world we live in. We do not have the logical development of our brain the same way we do as adults to interpret the world. As adults we have the ability to analyze what we're seeing in our conscious mind, and decide whether or not to accept it as truth. From birth to about age 8 we simply associate everything into being either positive or negative, and that information is directly stored in our subconscious mind.

Are you afraid of heights? Think you need to work hard to earn money? That all the good people are taken and you'll never find love? All rich people are crooks? Believe it's better not to make friends, because people just let you down? There's a good chance any beliefs like these you have come from your parents, guardians, teachers, during your early years, albeit unknowingly, who instilled these beliefs in you while your mind was still only taking information in and not able to filter it. For example, perhaps Jane Doe see's money as the root of all evil, if we go back in time to when she was a child we find out that money was a hot topic often fought about between her parents. In her child's mind, Jane Doe came to associate money as being bad, imprinting the belief: Money = Fighting = I can never have love if I have money.

The good news? We can reprogram our subconscious mind!

With our conscious mind now fully developed and able to rationalize, we can go back and review old belief patterns and decide if they do or don't serve us in our lives. One of the easiest ways to start to de-weed our subconscious garden is to look to the areas of your life in which you are feeling struggle, maybe there are many, or maybe one specific area stands out that brings you a great deal of stress and frustration.

Think back to your childhood and the views in your household on that area, and if any specific incidents come to mind (if you have multiple areas to work on then write them all down and do this process one at a time). Ask yourself:

- How did my parents feel about _____ ?
- Was there conflict about this in my home growing up?
- Did anything negative happen around this topic?
- How do I feel when I think about this?
- When did I start feeling this way?
- Does feeling this way support my current goals and aspirations?

Understanding why we feel and think the way we do about major areas of our life allows us to let those old beliefs go. Once you determine why you created that belief, you're free to release it, knowing that you picked it up at a time when you didn't have the logic to realize it wasn't what you wanted to imprint in your life. It is perfectly normal to feel some push back from your subconscious in letting go of these old thought patterns, and it will take time to imprint your new thought pattern in its place. You'll find those old beliefs bubble up into your mind, and you'll need to consciously take a moment to stop the thought, release it, and reaffirm your new belief.

Let's go through this process with the example of Jane Doe and her struggles around money, an issue many have struggles with. Jane Doe would go through it like this:

- How did my parents feel about money?
    - My father worked full time, my mom was a stay at home mom, so money was tight. My mom and dad often argued about how they were spending their money and how there was never enough savings. Mom wanted to shop, dad wanted to pay off debt, making it a source of tension when it was discussed.
- Was their conflict about this in my home growing up?
    - Often mom and dad would fight about money. Dad would always get angry

and yell things like "Where did it all go?"

- Did anything specific negative situation around this topic?
  - One-time mom took me on a shopping spree, and we had a wonderful day together, but when we arrived home with all of our bags of precious treasures dad flipped out. He yelled at mom for spending too much. I just wanted to go take everything back.
- How do I feel when I think about this?
  - My heart feels heavy, I have a pit in my stomach, and all I want is a hug.
- When did I start feeling this way?
  - The day of the shopping spree really was the turning point for my feelings about money.
- Does feeling this way support my current goals and aspirations?
  - No, it doesn't. Not having money doesn't make me happy or more

loved, it stresses me out. Being broke all the time makes it so I'm not able to enjoy doing things with my family that I want to do, like going on vacations to create new memories.

- Will letting re-writing this old thought pattern help me reach my goals?
  - o Yes. I realize that money isn't bad, and that having it doesn't mean I can't be loved. I realize I can have money in my life and love at the same time, and my old belief came from misinterpreting a situation as a child.

Now that Jane Doe has discovered the source of her belief, she's ready to let it go:

"I recognize that this old belief doesn't serve me anymore, and I am ready to release it."

And to re-program herself with a new affirmation:

"I am worthy of money AND love."

Now it's your turn! Use this process above to move through each area you are feeling struggle in. Take as much time as you need to sift through these feelings, and uncover where they stemmed from. Recognize them for what they really are: misinterpretations of situations or imprints of your parent's/guardian's beliefs that do not resonate with who you are now. Release each one and replace it with a positive affirmation.

You will continue to use these affirmations daily, and anytime your subconscious creeps in with the old belief, you'll quickly release that thought isn't what you want, and can cut it off like this, "I see this as my old thought pattern, thank you for sharing, but that's not who I am anymore! I am worthy of money AND love!" You'll notice that the old beliefs crop up less and less, until your new belief has firmly rooted itself as your new way of being!

This new belief system will support you as you embark on the journey using the Law of Attraction. Your subconscious is what communicates to the Universe, so you need it to be on the same page as what you consciously desire. If your subconscious says "having money makes me a bad person," but you're consciously saying, "I want money," your subconscious will win every time. Your subconscious mind wants above all to be safe and loved, it's trying to protect you, so don't get angry about these old beliefs you're moving through and releasing; your pal, the subconscious, was just trying to take care of you the only way it knew how!

Having your conscious and subconscious in alignment means we can move forward through this process unhindered! Get ready to embark on a journey that will show you just how powerful you really are! You are the creator of your reality; let's get cooking!

Over the next 3 weeks we will put the power of the Law of Attraction into play, creating daily habits that will allow you to define your reality, and above all, find much more joy! Are you ready? Let's do this!

What to Expect & Prep for the 2 Week Law of Attraction Retreat:

- Work through releasing old unsupportive belief patterns
- Work on choosing new supportive belief patterns
- Getting clear on what you really want to manifest

- Instilling daily habits to put you in sync with attracting what you really want
- Living your happiest life through gratitude

What You'll need:

- Set aside approximately 30 minutes a day to read through and practice each day's lesson.
- OPTIONAL: Get a journal, or set up a word document on your computer, to go through this course work. If you know you're more likely to do the work if you structure yourself to write things down then follow this method. If you know you are more likely to read the lesson but skip the work if you must write things down, you can do most of it in your mind.

For some people writing things down takes them out of the moment, disconnecting them from their emotions, and feelings are an important aspect of manifestation. If you wish to write during the course but notice you're in your head thinking more than feeling when you write, simply finish writing the lesson out, then review what you've wrote, and get back into your body and your heart with those thoughts.

NOTE: I will indicate if there is something that needs to be written down for future use.

Pre-work Alignment & What you REALLY Want!

In your Introduction to the Law of Attraction course, you began to work through our old belief patterns, and started to become aware of, and let go of, those that no longer serve who you want to become. As we move forward, continue to be aware of any feelings of doubt or fear that arise; and keep tracing these back to those old belief patterns and let them go.

The Law of Attraction allows you to build your own reality; you are the creator! This is a very exciting prospect; however, do you know what you *REALLY* want? So often in life we've been shot down, told to get our head out of the clouds, to be more practical, to compromise; and after years and years of being told these things we stop thinking big scale. We become afraid to dream big! In addition to that, it can be all too easy to get caught up living a dream that's not your own; for example, the quintessential "American Dream," sweeps so many people up in North America. The ideal of the beautiful house and white picket fence, the adoring family, the secure 9-5 job, the nice car;

not a bad dream IF that's what you really want. The trouble? A lot of people achieve these things and then feel empty; it wasn't what their heart really longed for.

So, before we start manifesting, you need to get really clear about what it is that makes your heart ba-boom! When you think about what you really want, deep down, you feel a rush, your pulse picks up, and you tingle with excitement! It is a rush!

Now, this may take some soul searching. Those dreams of yours might be loooooong buried from years of being told "no," or that those dreams are "ridiculous," or "impractical."

BEWARE THE CRABS

There's this phenomenon known as the Crab Mentality; and the first time I heard this I almost didn't believe it. It just sounded so absurd, but this is exactly what human beings do to each other...

When crabs walk into a top-open trap, lured in by bait OR if they're simple being held in an open bucket after they've been collected out of a trap, they will not escape.

They are perfectly capable of escaping, it is very easy for them to climb out, but they won't.

What happens? Why don't they try to escape?

Once a crab crawls into the trap to eat the bait, other crabs follow its lead, even after the bait is gone! Crabs have a group mentality, and mirror behavior. Then, when a crab tries to leave the trap, the other crabs will pull it back down. If the crab continues to try to crawl out of the trap, the other crabs will crush its claws, or rip off its limps. If it still persists, the other crabs will kill it.

When I first learned that my jaw dropped. The crab mentality is "If I can't have it, neither can you."

As you embark of a path of change, embracing your true strengths, and breaking away from the heard, you're going to see the Crab Effect. People might call you crazy, ridicule your dreams, all behind the misleading kind words "I'm just trying to look out for you."

Why does this happen?

When you march to the beat of your own drum, and pursue your dreams, it's like you're holding up a mirror to all those around you, that shows them they could be doing more, accomplishing more, living their wildest dreams; but they're not. Their inner "crab" comes out and they try to pull you back down, because it's easier for them to destroy your dream then to try to live their own.

You need to know this so that, 1. you don't let yourself be pulled down, AND 2. you don't take any of it personally, their words are a reflection of their own feelings of inadequacy.

Maybe you've experienced this crab effect, and you've locked away that long lost dream to avoid the cruel behavior of those people. It's time to dig it up. Feel it out; does that dream still make your heart jump for joy?! If so, now is the time.

You can be, and do, anything you want. Your only limits are in your beliefs. Change your thoughts, and change your life!

Pre-work

Grab a pen and a piece of paper and write out all of your goals and dreams your heart desires; then narrow down your list to 10 incredible things so amazing that, if they all happened within the next year, you'd be flabbergasted and jumping for joy! **This will be your Top 10 Manifestation List**!

Notice yourself holding back from writing something down? Something that feels "scary" or "impossible"? Push through and write it out. That's your old fear belief telling you it's "too big"; but nothing is too big to put on your list. You are a being of infinite potential and you can have it all!

A little story before we begin:
Thank you for the Burnt Pot

Last night I was cooking dinner, and I had some quinoa simmering away in a pot. It was almost ready and I turned the dial up to high to speed it along, then I went to the basement to clean the cat litter quickly. I came back upstairs, went to the washrooms to wash my hands, then went and sat on the couch with my husband.

About 15 minutes later my husband asks me, "Did you make tea?" I replied "No," and was confused why he asked. Then about 10 seconds later I clued in that the toasted smell he was asking about was my quinoa burning! With a fire under my butt I ran into the kitchen, snatched the pot off the stove and turned the burner off. I quickly grabbed a spoon and moved the top layer of quinoa back to see a blackened pot at the bottom, severely burnt. I calmly scooped the quinoa out and soaked the pot.

Now; if this had happened a few years ago I would have been cussing, and screaming, and crying about it. I would have declared that dinner was ruined (not really though, most of the quinoa was salvageable), that the pot was ruined (again, not really, just needed a scrub with steel wool), I would have been mad at myself... it would have completely ruined my day!

Instead, last night I calmly dealt with the situation, and after the initial shock, I was grateful for the burnt pot. It was a reminder from the Universe for me to slow down. No one got hurt, nothing got ruined, and I was reminded of a very important lesson; trying to rush things before they're ready isn't the way to go!

When gratitude becomes our way of life, the entire journey of life becomes a dream! When you can be grateful for what would have once made you upset, you're in tune with the Universe, and able to learn the lessons it has for you, instead of fighting against them.

Now get ready to embark on this life-changing journey!

Day 1: Gratitude is The Key; When you Wake up & Before you Sleep

In your introduction to The Law of Attraction you learned that no matter what you're thinking, you're drawing more of that to you; the good, the bad, and the ugly. So, in order to bring more of what we want into our lives, we need to come from a place of gratitude.

Gratitude is the Key!

A grateful heart has no space for fear or worry. Gratitude is the fastest way to turn negative thoughts around. It is your secret weapon to building your dream life! The more you are thankful, the happier you will feel, and like a magnet, you'll draw more circumstances to be grateful for!

In our modern lives, instant gratification has placed most of us in a state of expectation. We take things for granted, and worse off, if what we expect isn't delivered, we're fuming! It's left most people feeling miserable and hard done by and that there's never enough, when in fact, we should be rejoicing about all of the miraculous things in our lives!

The other issue we tend to run into as human beings is getting so focused in on our own lives that we're not seeing the bigger picture. We tend to get tunnel vision around what's happening in our own lives; this is excellent when we need to focus in and get things done, but it can be very overwhelming if we don't remember to take a step back for some much-needed perspective. When our immediate life is all we're seeing, our tasks can feel monumental, and it can leave us feeling powerless, which couldn't be further from the truth.

Today we are going to take a big step back and see things as they really are, to gain perspective, and to instill gratitude as our go-to the next time we get tunnel vision and forget that we are bigger than our day to day activities. We will be introducing our first TWO daily habits today, that are so simple, yet so powerful, that they can change your life. These two daily habits you will continue to do each day for the rest of this course (and hopefully every day afterwards too!).

Habit # 1 Morning Gratitude: 10 Things I'm Grateful For

Have you ever woken up in the morning, you had a good night's rest, you're feeling good, then you get out of bed a stub your toe? It hurts like hell, and you're upset, asking "Why did this happen to me?" and the entire day seems to go downhill from there. Everything that could go wrong does. By the time midday rolls around you're just wishing the day was over, you're ready to crawl into bed and forget the entire day? It's happened to all of us.

Your mind is like a magnet, so after you got hurt, and upset, and dwelled on it, you were telling the Universe to send you more stuff to be upset about. None of us consciously want more stuff to complain about, but what you focus on expands. Now – to clarify – this doesn't mean you can't stub your toe, feel the pain, say a few profanities, and get it out of your system; it's when we dwell on the thought that we run into drawing more to us. Scream, cry, yell, do whatever you need to do in the moment, and then consciously decide to let it go and replace it with gratitude, "Well my foot hurts now BUT I'm grateful that I have a foot; some people don't."

Why did I use this analogy? Because what happens to you in the beginning of your day sets you up for success or failure for the rest of your day. It makes your first thoughts the most important ones of your day. If something small like stubbing your toe can completely derail your day, imagine how something consciously done, like gratitude in the morning, can profoundly set your day up for joy and success!

10 Things I'm Grateful For is going to be your new habit that is going to set you up to be attracting what you want to you. I suggest you do this as the very first thing when you wake up in the morning, you can even do this before you get out of bed! Some people like to journal their list, however if journaling means you might not do it, then you can do this practice in your head. Each morning when you wake up you're going to immediately work through thinking about, and being grateful for, 10 different things. It is most important as you're moving through your list that you're feeling the gratitude, and the best way to do that is to expand on each item on why you're grateful:

"Thank you, Thank you, Thank you, for _____, because _____"

So, right about now you're probably thinking "OK, I can think of ten things for today, but 10 NEW things every day to be grateful for?! How will I do that?" This is where we break the tunnel vision, and gain perspective.

Do you have internet access? This incredible tool has allowed Earth to unite as a global community. It's created the free exchange of knowledge and wisdom, customs, and traditions, worldwide, wherever you are, at the click of a button. Think of all the connections you've made, the things you've learned, online shopping, and a million other little things the internet has simplified in our lives! *THANK YOU!*

Do you have access to food? It's incredible the orchestra of work that goes into bringing all of the variety of foods to us from around the globe! The farmers, the pickers, the packers, the distributors, the transporters, the sorters, the stockers; all working in harmony to provide you with access to a massive variety of foods! *Thank you!*

Do you have a house or apartment to live in? *Thank you!* Do you have access to clean, drinkable water? *Thank you!* Do you have electricity at the flick of a switch? *Thank you!* Do you have access to a vehicle or public transit? *Thank you!*

We live on a planet, just right to support life, the odds of which happening are absolutely staggering. We have trees that continuously replenish oxygen, the atmosphere held in by the ozone layer separating us from the vacuum of space. We're just the right distance from the sun to be warm enough to support life, and not too hot as to make life unbearable or impossible. We have an incredible abundance of water, that sustains all life on our planet. This incredibly rare set of variables is truly awe-inspiring; if any of them were off by even a fraction we would not be alive. *Thank you!*

How about your remarkable senses that allow you to experience this world? Taste, Touch, Smell, Sight, and Hearing give you the ability to interpret life, and experience all the joys of being alive! *Thank you, senses!*

There are limitless things to be grateful for, most often the things we take for granted are the things that bring so much pleasure into our day to day lives. Think about the last time your electricity went out, how heavily that impacted you. *Thank you for electricity!* We couldn't imagine life without it.

Here are some categories to help spark your imagination each day as you think of your 10 things to be Grateful for:

- Health
- Wealth
- Career
- Success
- Love
- Family
- Friends
- Pets
- Home
- Nature
- Senses
- Food & Water
- Utilities
- Experiences
- Knowledge
- Time
- Material things
- Humanitarian work
- Charities
- Human spirit

- Generosity

- Ecosystem

As you can see there are endless things to be grateful for, and the more you practice gratitude, the easier it will be to find things to be grateful for each new day!

A NOTE ON REPEATS: This is about feeling gratitude more than performing this task perfectly, so if you find yourself thankful for the same thing every few days, there's nothing wrong with that! In fact, sometimes kicking off with the things nearest and dearest to your heart can propel your thoughts to reach for more things to be grateful for! For example, you might be grateful for your kids, your spouse, or your pets, every single day as the first thing that comes to mind, and if that makes your heart jump for joy start off with them! If those are daily though, use them as a precursor to your 10; don't use them as an excuse to not look for more things to be grateful for.

Habit # 2 The Magic Bedtime:

The BEST thing that Happened Today

Just as we begin the day with gratitude we will end it with gratitude. When you make gratitude the very first thing you do in the morning, and the very last thing you do before bed, you set yourself up to experience incredible changes in your life. You're instilling these beliefs to your very core.

When you get into bed at night, before you go to sleep, think through your day, and be grateful for the best thing that happened that day! Through this process your mind has to search through all of the great things that happened during your day! Once you find the best thing that happened to you, say, or think, *"Thank you, Thank you, Thank you, for _____ it was amazing because _____!"*

It's that simple! Yet it will leave your spirits feeling uplifted, and your heart filled with joy, as your drift off to sleep. This makes us excited for each new day, as we begin to see all of the amazing things that happen in our lives! There are always things to be grateful for, it's just a matter of taking the time to recognize them!

Today's To-Do List:

- 10 things I'm Grateful For: Make a mental or written list of 10 things you're grateful for, and for each one complete the sentence: *"Thank you, Thank you, Thank you, for _____, because _____"*
  - As this is the day your learned this new habit, and may be later in the day that your read this, do you list of ten upon finishing today's reading. Starting tomorrow do this first thing in the morning.
- The Best Thing That Happened Today: Mentally go through your day looking for the best thing that happened to you. Once you've found the best thing, complete this sentence: *"Thank you, Thank you, Thank you, for _____ it was amazing because _____!"*

Day 2: Faith

One of the most challenging things to do is to relinquish our sense of control. So often we want something to happen in this very 'exact' way, that we're blind to all other possibilities. We only have so much perspective from our human vantage point, add to that an iron will to make something happen, and our field of view shrinks ever more.

As physical beings we can only see a small sliver of the playing field, and there are a million other possibilities and moving parts outside our realm of thought and vision. We can have access to these possibilities at any time, through our connection to the Universe. The catch? It's on faith; you do not get to know 'how', and hence, must relinquish your desire to control every detail.

The Law of Attraction needs room to work. If Ted decides "I want a promotion at work, and the only way I'm going to get it by making a proposal about how to save the company 5% this next quarter," he might be missing the Universe attempting to show him that his friend and co-worker Steve, the guy in a higher up position he wants, is moving to another department and making recommendations for a replacement. But Ted is so focused on this proposal idea, dead set in his mind it's the only way to get his promotion, he entirely missed the opportunity to talk to Steve about how he wanted that promotion.

Or Jenny, who is head over heels in love with the guy who works at her favorite coffee shop. She's determined that "He is the one!" even though he forgets her name every day, and she has absolutely nothing in common with him. Being so fixated on that one person, she misses out on the cute hipster nerdy guy that's 100% right for her that's sitting one table over.

Your job is to know what you want, the Universe will guide you from there in how to get it. This is what is referred to as the 'Surrender,' when we decide what we want then, trust and believe in the Universe bringing it into our lives. This can feel frustrating, especially if you're a perfectionist or a control freak; but it's also thrilling! Once you experience it, how easily and effortlessly your dream manifests, you'll be hooked for more!

So, what should our promotion seeker and hopeless romantic have done instead?

VISUALIZING THE OUTCOME

The Universe responds to thoughts and feelings, making the most powerful thing you can do visualizing the outcome you want, in vivid detail, and feel what it feels like to accomplish that outcome as if it's already happened, and to be grateful for it before it's occurred. If it's tangible to your mind, the Universe must provide it physically. The more detail, the more gratitude, and the more feeling you have about it, the better.

Let's use our example of Ted to see what he should have done to put the law of attraction to use for himself:

Ted decides he wants a promotion, so he begins to imagine receiving it. Ted pictures himself going in to work like every normal day, getting the call from his boss to go to his office. Ted imagines walking into the office and sitting down across from his boss, his boss smiling and congratulating him as he explains to Ted he got the position. Ted imagines how amazing he'll feel in that moment, elated and excited, and the firm hand shake from his boss. Ted then imagines moving into his own office, the feeling of accomplishment sweeping over him. He pictures how he'll set his desk up and what he'll decorate the office with. He is full of contentment. Ted finishes his visualization by saying, "Thank you, thank you, thank you for this incredible promotion, because it makes me feel valued!"

The Universe will then begin moving people and events into place to bring this into fruition. Ted may still have the idea for the proposal, and that might be the actionable step he starts off with, but he isn't dead set on the idea that as the only way to get the promotion. Ted simply knows the end game he wants and is beginning to do what he can to work his way there. The Universe could line him up in many different ways for the promotion now, because it's free to show him the available paths; Ted is open minded enough to see them now!

In Jenny's case, she imagines the qualities she wants in her ideal partner, caring, thoughtful, & artsy. She pictures going out on dates together, and spending time doing activities together that she gets excited about. She imagines how wonderful it is to feel loved, for who she is. She imagines what it'll be like sharing her life with this person. Jenny finishes his visualization by saying, "Thank you, thank you, thank you for this amazing partner, because I am worthy of love!"

Just like with Ted, The Universe now has the room to work, to set Jenny into alignment with who she's trying to meet. The key in both cases is to get good and clear about what you want, and trust the how to the Universe!

FAITH

The Law of Attraction takes a leap of faith, this can be hard in the beginning and extremely exciting once you're used to how it works. Basically, you're placing your order with the Universe, by seeing that end game result and being grateful for it in advance. How and when that comes to you, is up to the Universe; it's a bit of a game! Now it's important to remember time is relative, in our existence we tend to be obsessed with time. The Universe can work to move things in to place instantly, and it is shocking how fast things can manifest for you.

Now, this instant response system of the universe works both ways, which is why you gotta work on that faith muscle! If you want to manifest $5000 for your dream vacation, you do your visualization, you're all in a tizzy about how incredible it's going to be, and the Universe starts to move into action, "Dream vacation, you got it, babe!" But then, doubt creeps in your mind, thoughts like "Ugh, but that IS a lot of money," and "I have so many bills, I'm so broke," and the Universe says, "Ok, lots of debt and bills on its way!" And then you refocus on the vacation, and then doubt and fear, flip flopping back and forth, and the Universe is sitting there, pulling their hair, screaming "Make up your mind! What do you want?!"

Now, we are all human after all, and the goal isn't to never have a fear or doubt pop up, though with practice you'll find those thoughts significantly diminish in your life. The goal is to not dwell on those thoughts, to develop your awareness so you notice when those thoughts pop up, and auto-correct yourself. For example, when the above thought came up "Ugh, but that IS a lot of money," instead of sitting in that feeling, we take note that's cropped up due to an old underlying belief about money, we stop right away, and redirect, "But money is just energy, like I am; it's a tool to get me to my goal, and I am capable and deserving of manifesting this money."   The more you catch yourself in the middle of a negative thought, and redirect it to the positive, the easier and more aware you'll become of your thoughts.

TEST OF FAITH

The test of faith is something that can happen anytime during the manifesting process, and usually crops up when you're working on manifesting something that feels very BIG to you. Maybe it's getting a new business off the ground, trying to manifest 1 million dollars, looking for the perfect love; the Universe will test your faith. You'll never know when, or how, and it's usually very challenging to persevere through it. It's when most people give up, because all signs are pointing to *no*, everything that could have gone wrong did, and you're left with no idea how to salvage the situation.

The Universe is testing your faith, and it's one BIG MF test! For example, maybe you start a new business, you invest your life savings, you got all your ducks in a row, the manufacturer's lined up, employees hired, and you found the perfect location for your warehouse. The day after your product arrives, a pipe leaks overnight, and your warehouse is flooded, and your merchandise is soaked and ruined. You're screaming bloody murder (you're human, it's ok to freak out a little) you have no idea how to make this right, there's no money left to re-order all the merchandise, all signs point to 'quit'. The only thing you have left is your faith, focusing on the end game, visualizing, and trusting that the Universe has your back.

Right when you're at your limit, and your faith is the only thing left standing, somehow, someway, everything will come together, as if by magic. Maybe an investor out of nowhere, maybe an insurance check, maybe someone wants to buy out your product patent; whatever the case may be, the Universe will carry you through *IF* you keep believing.

VISUALIZATION EXERCISE

It's time to pull out your List of the Top 10 Things you want to Manifest. You're going to pick 3 things from your list and visualize each one as if you've just achieved it. Get into as much detail, as much feeling, and as much gratitude about each one as possible! Where are you? Who are you with? What can you smell, taste, touch, see, and hear? How do you feel? How did you get the news? Really get into the moment! When you've done this exercise on each of your 3 choices you should feel elated.

Today's To-Do List:

- First thing in the Morning do your 10 things I'm Grateful For: Make a mental or written list of 10 things you're grateful for, and for each one complete the sentence: *"Thank you, Thank you, Thank you, for* _____, *because* _____ *"*

- *Pick 3 items from your Top 10 manifestation list, and use the Visualization practice above on each of the 3 you've chosen. Get into as much detail and feeling as possible.*

- The Best Thing That Happened Today: Mentally go through your day looking for the best thing that happened to you. Once you've found the best thing, complete this sentence: *"Thank you, Thank you, Thank you, for* _____ *it was amazing because* _____ *!"*

Day 3: Affirmations

Affirmations can be one of your best tools to redirect negative thoughts and reprogram your beliefs. They are easy to pull out at any given moment; and they can be a great way to round out your morning gratitude practice. At any moment you can use an affirmation to replace a negative thought, to empower yourself if fear or doubt creep up, and to anchor in moments of success. You can make up your own affirmations, or use any of the ones below that you feel resonate with you.

Today I'll be sharing some of my favorite affirmations, you will try them out, and see which ones feels right, or use them as guidelines for creating your own. It's important that an affirmation also feels natural and can be effortlessly recalled; if you're stumbling to find the words it will take you out of the moment.

Turning your Top 10 Manifestation List into Affirmations

This is a very simple and fun place to begin! Just like with our visualization exercise, we want to see our top 10 Manifestation List as if it's already achieved. This takes it out of the future tense and into the present or, in a few cases, past tense (this tends to relate to short term events). You're going to take your list and re-write it as if they have all happened, and this will be your new list. So, for example if one of your top 10 is, "I'd like to find a romantic partner," that would become "I am in a romantic relationship."

Another few examples:

"I want to earn a million dollars," Becomes, "I am a millionaire."

"I want to finish writing my book," Becomes, "I am a New York times bestselling author."

"I want to vacation in Hawaii with my husband," Becomes, "My husband and I had the most incredible vacation in Hawaii."

Now grab your lists and start rewriting it!

Go-To Affirmations

These are my favorite affirmations. Read through and see if any of them feel right for you, and if they do, write them down, or repeat them a few times until you remember it. While affirmations can be as long as you want, keeping it simple and short means it will be easier to conjure up a moment's notice. If you're too busy thinking about what the heck the words were, you won't be feeling it in the moment, which is the real key to them. You could also tack two of them together if you like!

W E A L T H

"I am a money magnet!"

"Money comes to me easily and effortlessly!"

"Money is all around me!"

"I have the mind of a millionaire!"

"Universe, I am ready and willing to receive any and all of your blessings!"

"Thank you for the unexpected income!"

H E A L T H

"I am in perfect health!"

"My body feels energized and young!"

"I have tons of energy!"

"I am pain free!"

You can get specific with this, if you have something health wise you're currently struggling with, make an affirmation about how it is in a perfect state. For example, I was starting to experience motion sickness when I was watching certain video games and movies on new televisions with motion "smoothing" features. I started to believe "I get motion sickness," and then I was experiencing it all the time. I realized we have the power to change our bodies down to the cellular level, so one night while I was experiencing motion sickness I started to repeatedly tell myself, "I do not get motion sickness, I feel great." While at first it felt like a lie, I kept on thinking it over and over until the motion sickness literally disappeared, and I've never experienced it again since.

We have all heard of people curing cancer or terminal illness through changing their thoughts; there really are no limits. It can be challenging, especially if you're feeling ill, to believe you are well, but practice it. Sometimes it can help to start with something small, to show yourself that it is possible.

CAREER

"I am a successful _____!"

"Opportunities come to me effortlessly!"

"Thank you for the unexpected customers!"

"Thank you for the unexpected orders!"

"Thank you for the unexpected raise!"

L O V E

"I am loved."

"I am surrounded by love."

"I have romance in my life!"

"Fun, romantic, spontaneous things happen to me often!"

R E L A T I O N S H I P S

"I have incredible friends!"

"I am surrounded by like-minded people!"

"I have the best relationship with _____!"

As you can see with affirmations you can be as specific or open with them as you wish! I always make sure to be thankful for the unexpected, every single day, to allow the Universe the opportunity to bring things into my life I didn't even realize I wanted! Just like our faith practice, it helps you to relinquish control and watch the magic reveal itself to you!

Choose at least 2-3 affirmations for the list above (or create your own) to begin using daily. They can be all in one area you're working on, or a mix if you wish to improve your mindset in multiple areas. At least once a day consciously say your affirmations, and then during the day when negativity or doubt creeps up around the topic, let the negative thought go and say your new affirmation, which will begin to implant the new belief.

Today's To-Do List:

- First thing in the Morning do your 10 things I'm Grateful For: Make a mental or written list of 10 things you're grateful for, and for each one complete the sentence: *"Thank you, Thank you, Thank you, for _____, because _____"*

- Re-write your 10 Top Manifestation List as if those things have already manifested.

- Choose at least 2-3 affirmations to begin using on a daily basis to instill those new beliefs.

- The Best Thing That Happened Today: Mentally go through your day looking for the best thing that happened to you. Once you've found the best thing, complete this sentence: *"Thank you, Thank you, Thank you, for _____ it was amazing because _____!"*

Day 4: Placing your Cosmic Order!

Today we're going to have some fun! You're going to put in your 'order' with the Universe, and simultaneous we are going to work on strengthening your faith muscle! The hardest part is just going to be choosing what you want!

The Universe brings our thoughts into physical form; we're constantly placing orders with our thoughts, the trick is that we want to be consciously placing the orders we *actually* want. We've already learned that the Universe doesn't discern want from don't want, so we must think about the situation or thing we want. The Universe brings more of what we're thinking about to us. Thinking about bills? More bills are bound to show up. Thinking you never have enough time? You're bound to get busier. So be sure to be mindful of your thoughts.

The other thing to watch out for is cancelling out what you want when fear or doubt sneak up. Remember, your affirmations are your arsenal to quickly reaffirm your new beliefs and to stamp out those old fears and doubts before they take you off course. The more you practice them, the more aware of your thoughts you'll become.

Our first step today, is of course, figuring out what you want to order! There's no item too big or too small; you can literally ask for anything you want. If you can dream it, the Universe can provide it! For our purposes today, I want you to think of something that you believe, whole heartedly, can show up in your life in the next couple weeks, but that would also be incredible! There's no room for doubt in the equation.

Get really excited about it, and then place your order! You can do this out loud, or in your head, whatever helps you feel the joy and excitement more.

"Dear Universe, I'm placing an order with you for _____. When I think about _____ my heart races, and I get all excited! Receiving _____ makes me fell _____! Thank you, thank you, thank you, for _____!"

Next, you're going to use the visualization practice you learned, and imagine receiving your order. Imagine how you feel, who told you the news, what your senses pick up; all those wonderous details that make it real. Feel all the gratitude you can for receiving it.

Lastly, we're going to make an affirmation to use daily for your order. This is going to firmly implant the belief that your order is coming to fruition. You'll use this at the end of your morning 10 gratitude's, when you're already in a state of joy and gratitude, for things you already have. Saying this at that time affirms this is in your life: "Thank you, thank you, thank you, for _____!"

Today's To-Do List:

- First thing in the Morning do your 10 things I'm Grateful For: Make a mental or written list of 10 things you're grateful for, and for each one complete the sentence: *"Thank you, Thank you, Thank you, for _____, because _____"*

- Place your Order with the Universe for something you want to manifest within the next few weeks

- Do the visualization exercise for your order

- Say or think your affirmation on your order: *"Thank you, thank you, thank you, for _____"*

- Remember to use your daily affirmations

- The Best Thing That Happened Today: Mentally go through your day looking for the best thing that happened to you. Once you've found the best thing, complete this sentence: *"Thank you, Thank you, Thank you, for _____ it was amazing because _____!"*

Day 5: The Manifesting Formula

Manifesting becomes simplified when we understand that there is an actual formula involved, and once we know that process we have the steps we need to proceed. Our non-physical world creates our physical world. The popular, "Thoughts Become Things," quote is something most people have heard of, but it's rather vague.

As you learned in the introduction, your beliefs govern your thoughts. Your beliefs live in your subconscious mind, and your subconscious mind is your connection to the Universe, your communicator. We know this is the root of all we create; so, if our subconscious mind and conscious mind are not in alignment, the subconscious will win.

We've been working on installing new beliefs in your subconscious, through consciously letting go of old thought patterns, and through replacing them with affirmations of what you want your new beliefs to be. While this is a work in progress, now that you have been aware of your thought patterns for several days in a row you should be noticing the beginning of a shift in your thinking.

But there is more to the formula than this! Your beliefs are the foundation of the process, but there's much more to it, and each step is just as vital!

The Manifesting Formula looks like this:

Beliefs > Thoughts > Emotions >Actions > Results

How the formula works:

Your beliefs (subconscious) govern your thoughts (conscious), our thoughts create our emotions and how we feel about what we're thinking, and those emotions propel us into taking action. Action is the bridge between the non-physical and the physical, firmly grounding your thoughts in your visible reality. When you take action you also strengthen your beliefs, because you're seeing what you're thinking about as even more real and attainable than when you just thought about it. Through acting you will find that you will be answered with your desired results. Plans, people, and opportunities will present themselves in ways you never imagined, bringing your thoughts into the physical world.

Beliefs are your Foundation

Your beliefs are the entire foundation of everything you will ever manifest. Just like building a home, we must start with ensuring our foundation is sturdy enough to support what we want to build. Examine your beliefs, and pay special attention to negative thoughts that creep into your mind. They are your indicators of beliefs in conflict with what you aspire to be/create.

Thoughts are your Creator

Your thoughts are your creations. If you're thinking about it, be prepared for it to soon arrive in your life! This gives the saying 'be mindful' a whole new level of meaning! If you are dwelling on things that do not bring you joy, consciously begin to think of the opposite which you'd like to replace it with.

Emotions are your Thermometer

Your emotions tell you exactly what you need to know. Ask yourself, "Is what I'm thinking about in alignment with what I REALLY want?" Your feelings are a dead giveaway. Do you feel excited and happy by what you're thinking? Not feeling much? Feeling unhappy? These are all crucial indicators. It's important when we manifest we make sure that we are manifesting OUR ideal life; not the life your parents, your friends, your co-workers, or society wants for you – the life YOU want for you. Trust your feelings. When you are lit on fire with excitement, and joy, at the thought of the life you're creating, no force can stop you!

Action is the Bridge

When you're feeling enthusiastic about the life you're creating, it will urge you into action. You will be so excited, so ecstatic, that you simply cannot sit still! The action you take will root your beliefs in what you are creating even more strongly in your subconscious mind as well, making it simple to keep your mind focused on it.

We're going to spend some time discussing action further now, because it is a crucial component, and often over looked and misunderstood, when it comes to manifesting. It's not our job to know the HOW, but then what action do we take? This often stumps people directly into doing nothing. While yes, you're not supposed to know the how, you need to start bringing the non-physical into the physical, to use your excitement and energy, to bring forth your desire. You're telling the Universe, "I trust this is going to happen!" when you begin to take action. That means doing something at first that moves you towards that goals, and being completely open to signs and signals on where to go with it next.

It's important to trust your gut feeling when it comes to action; you'll have huge motivation to act, so what's the first thing that comes to mind? Go start doing it. You can course correct as needed, so don't judge or overthink what your impulse is. The Universe will find a way to communicate with you about where to go from there to you, no matter what your choice is.

Maybe you feel inspired to go take a walk as your action, you have no idea how this is going to help you in any way, but on that walk, you meet someone, or see something, or get a phone call, or have an epiphany, that leads you to exactly what you need! Or maybe you decide to just start doing some online research and you stumble onto exactly the right information you need. Or maybe you just start brainstorming and writing down ideas, or buy a book, or drive home a new way from work – the thing is, it doesn't matter WHAT you start doing, just follow your gut and do it! You'll be surprised how fast the Universe intervenes and shows you the next step on your path.

ACTION VS INSPIRED ACTION

The action you need to take could be big or very small; the trick is that you listen inside for a nudge to do something. This is how you can tell the difference between action and inspired action. If you feel compelled to do something, you can't explain why, and perhaps it doesn't even necessarily have anything to do with your manifestation goal (that you can see), follow the nudge. It may be clear as day or make no sense, but you need to see where it leads you.

This is where your faith comes in, in trusting the process, and seeing where the path takes you. If you're not sure if you're moving from Inspired Action or just simply Acting because you don't trust the way to be revealed, use your feelings as a compass:

INSPIRED ACTION:

- Acting out of Excitement
- Acting from the feeling of a Gentle Nudge
- Acting because it makes you feel Happy
- Acting because it inexplicably feels Right

ACTION:

- o   Acting to Force your Dream to Manifest
- o   Acting out of Fear of Doubt
- o   Acting when is makes you feel Uncomfortable*
- o   Acting when you feel nervous

*A NOTE ABOUT COMFORT

There's "This feels wrong," discomfort, and there's, "That's big and scary," discomfort. The first is a sign that what you're doing isn't right, that it's not in line with your values, and will leave you feeling upset. The second, the big and scary kind, is the type of discomfort that pushes us past the edges of our comfort zones in a way that makes us grow. The second type is a good kind of discomfort, and one we need to embrace. By pushing the boundaries of our comfort zone, we learn what seemed 'scary' is actually incredible!

Think back to when you first decided to try something new, perhaps when you first learned how to ride a bike without the training wheels. It was scary, you made sure your parent/guardian/friend was holding onto the back of your seat for support. You were scared that you might topple over, and not sure you'd be able to do it. You stopped and started a few times, and slowly got the hang of it, pushing past the fear and focusing on the activity.

Suddenly you're riding with no one holding your seat, you feel free, flying down the road at an incredible speed! You're empowered, knowing you accomplished this. As time passes you get better and better with you bike, and you can't imagine life before you rode it.

This is how we continue to grow and experience new things in life, and show fear whose boss! As you continue to do new things that at first feel 'uncomfortable', you'll expand the range of your comfort zone, and have more and more incredible things In your life. So, if you're feeling discomfort, ask yourself if it feels somehow wrong, morally, ethically, or if it's a force of will negating your trust in the Universe, OR, is it the kind of discomfort that is from it being outside of your comfort zone, which is forcing you to grow? Let your intuition guide you.

REMEMBER: Nothing new ever grows inside of your Comfort Zone.

Results are the Rewards

Last, but not least, are the results; as your vision comes into fruition. After you've followed this manifestation formula, your thoughts will begin to take form in the real world before your eyes. You'll see the pieces of the puzzle fall into place, and your dream realized. The amount of time this takes can be instant, or it could take time, but as you keep focusing on it and working toward it, it will come to fruition.

Today's Task: Using the Manifestation Formula!

It's time to pull out your top 10 Manifestation List again! I want you to look over your list and pick the #1 Desire off your list! This might be the desire that makes your heart race extra fast when you think about it, or the 1 thing that helps most of your other come to fruition (the domino effect!). For example, let's say this is your list:

1. I own a home on the beach
2. I vacation in Tahiti with my family
3. I have fallen in love with my soul mate
4. I retired from my 9 to 5 job
5. I am earning over $5000 a week from home
6. I wrote a best-selling novel
7. I have lots of free time daily for my favorite hobbies, reading, hiking, and knitting
8. I am able to donate $10,000 a year to my favorite charity

9. I own a Ferrari

10. I am debt free

Looking of this list, Manifestation #5, jumps out as what will unlock many of the other desires on this list. Earning $5000 a week would allow 2, 4, 7, 8, and 9 to happen, and put 10 in the running to come to pass as well. However, it's important to consider that #6 could be the catalyst to make #5 happen! Again, this comes back to not needing to know the 'how,' and simply in helping guide you into picking what you want to manifest first! Don't overthink it, simply have some fun and follow your intuition! The most important thing is when you think about achieving whichever one you pick that it lights your heart on fire!

Using what you've learned, search yourself to see that your beliefs are in line with your goal. Do any doubts of fears creep up? If so release them, and replace them with new beliefs (you can use affirmations here) that support your new way of thinking. Next think about the goal, use visualization and gratitude about receiving it. Let those thoughts inspire you, and ignite your emotions! Listen for any inner nudges to take action, and follow them!

Today's To-Do List:

- First thing in the Morning do your 10 things I'm Grateful For: Make a mental or written list of 10 things you're grateful for, and for each one complete the sentence: *"Thank you, Thank you, Thank you, for _____, because _____"*

- Use the Manifestation Formula on your #1 Desire from your top 10 Manifestation List

- Say or think your affirmation on your Cosmic Order from Day 4: *"Thank you, thank you, thank you, for _____"*

- Remember to use your daily affirmations

- The Best Thing That Happened Today: Mentally go through your day looking for the best thing that happened to you. Once you've found the best thing, complete this sentence: *"Thank you, Thank you, Thank you, for _____ it was amazing because _____!"*

Day 6: The Magic Morning

Our first day we learned just how important starting off each day with a positive mindset and attitude is. You've been using gratitude to start off every day since then, to start bringing forth more of the good things into your life! We are going to have an extended morning routine that will leave you feeling incredibly happy and centered. This is going to start right when you get up in the morning, so read this practice today before you go to bed, and do it tomorrow. You will need some extra time in the morning for some aspects of this practice, so if tomorrow is a busy day be sure to set your alarm clock 40 – 60 minutes earlier.

You will need:

- A journal, notepad, or a piece of paper
- A pen or pencil
- A watch, timer, or smart phone
- Your top 10 manifestation list
- A book or article (can be from the web) on personal development.

UPON WAKING

As you wake up in the morning, take a moment to lay in bed, and slowly take in your surroundings. Breathe deeply, place one or both hands over your heart and smile. Say, "Thank you, thank you, thank you, for another day of being alive!" take another moment to sit in that feeling of gratitude, and then get out of bed.

YOUR MORNING ROUTINE

With every step you take as you go through your regular morning routine, say 'Thank you!' in your mind. Then, as you go about your routine, find as many things to be grateful for as you can! Getting dressed? "Thank you for all of my clothes!" Using the bathroom faucet, toilet, or shower? "Thank you for indoor plumbing!" Brushing your teeth? "Thank you for a clean mouth!" Making breakfast? "Thank you, fridge, for keeping my food fresh! Thank you, stove, for making cooking easy! Thank you, electricity, for powering everything!" Making coffee or tea? "Thank you for boiling water, this beverage makes my morning so much better!"

Whatever your morning routine, find all the little things to be grateful for!

CONSCIOUS CREATION

Once your basic morning routine is done, grab your writing tools, and your book or article, and find a quiet comfortable place to sit where you won't be disturbed. After you've settled, it's time to begin!

- Begin by doing your daily 10 things I'm grateful for list (written or in your mind).
- Next, pull out your Top 10 Manifestation list, and read through each of the items on your list, saying, "Thank you!" after reading each one.
- Pick up your Personal Development book or article and read for at least 15-20 minutes. Set your timer or alarm if you have a schedule to keep.
- Now close your eyes, and take 3 deep breathes. You're going to mentally go through your upcoming day, and be grateful in advance for all of the events before they happen. Be grateful for each thing going well, imagine how good it feels when everything in your day goes smoothly. Being thankful in advance is the surest way to have a remarkably good day!
- You can now reopen your eyes, and grab your journal or paper, and your writing utensil. Set your timer for

5 minutes, then ask yourself, "What would make me happy today?" and just start writing. Don't censor your thoughts, let yourself free write; we often repress what we want to do and focus on what we must do in life, and it's important to let yourself experience your hearts desires. It doesn't matter what comes up, it's simply important to let your thoughts come out. Once your timer goes off, re-read your list and choose one thing off of your list to do today to make yourself happy.

o Now it's time to meditate, to sit in purposeful silence, to center your mind and connect to the Universal Flow. Meditation is a practice about stilling the mind; notice the word 'practice', this takes work, and thoughts *will* bubble up. It's OK when they do, don't get angry, just gently release them. To meditate:

- Set your timer for 5 minutes. Sit cross legged and pay attention to your posture. Keep your neck in line with your spine, and sit up tall. Your hands can rest on top of your knees or thighs. Close your eyes, and focus in on your breath. Relax your body, and release any tension you're holding onto by breathing into that area, and exhaling the stress and tension away. Still your mind, and continue to focus in on your breathing. If you notice thoughts coming up, thank them, and let them go, and refocus in on the breathing. Just be. When your timer goes off, turn it off, then take one big inhale and slowly release it in an exhale. You should feel at peace afterwards.

- o Lastly, you're going to say your affirmations, and include, "Thank you for the unexpected news!" to your affirmations, allowing the Universe to bring new opportunities your way today.

After this Magic Morning practice, you should be feeling happy, elated, and excited for your day. It should give you a sense of serenity as well; evaporating any anxiety, doubt or fear. While this morning practice is more involve, you may feel so good after doing it that you wish to make it part of your daily routine! You can also pick and choose your favorite aspects of this Magic Morning to make your own customized routine.

Today's To-Do List:

- First thing in the Morning do your 10 things I'm Grateful For: Make a mental or written list of 10 things you're grateful for, and for each one complete the sentence: *"Thank you, Thank you, Thank you, for _____, because _____"*
- Follow the Magic Morning Practice as it's laid out
- Say or think your affirmation for your Cosmic Order from Day 4: *"Thank you, thank you, thank you, for _____"*
- Remember to use your daily affirmations
- The Best Thing That Happened Today: Mentally go through your day looking for the best thing that happened to you. Once you've found the best thing, complete this sentence: *"Thank you, Thank you, Thank you, for _____ it was amazing because _____!"*

Day 7: The Vision Board

A vision board is a fun way to engage your imagination, and focus on what you want to manifest. If visualization is a difficult practice for you, making a vision board with tangible images can help. For making your vision board you will need:

1. Bristol board, craft paper, or cardboard (2ft x 2ft or larger)
2. Scissors
3. Glue stick
4. Magazines, photos, and/or print outs
5. Photos of you/you and your loved ones/you and your friends

OR

1. Google Images and/or Pintrest
2. Photos of you/you and your loved ones/you and your friends
3. A Photo editor that can-do collages

This practice is a lot of fun, because you're basically placing a big order for what you want your future to look like in all areas of your life! You will get inspired as your browse through photographs, be it magazines or on the internet. Your Vision Board can be digital or physical. If you choose to do digital then you need to use that image as your phone lock screen, home screen, and your computers background image. Vision boards are meant to be viewed regularly, to solidify those images in your mind, and reinforce your manifestation of them into your life.

If you do a physical board, once it's done it's excellent to hang it in an office, or bedroom, where you'll look at it multiple times throughout the day. Whatever option you choose, the key is they you have it in a visible place for you. And – you can always do both if you wish!

So, our first step is to find the images we want to have as a part of our vision board! If you're making a physical board and want to use magazines primarily – if you have a bunch excellent, and if not head to the store to pick some up! You'll want to have a variety – look to pick up a travel, business, & home design magazine. If you're doing a digital board, you have the benefit of unlimited images to find on the web.

On your vision board you're going to want to have balance; meaning you'll want to see yourself flourishing in all areas of your life. Where are you travelling? What's your home look like? Does your home have a pool? Is it in the city, or the country? What's your dream car? What successes are you celebrating? What's your bank statement look like? Who are you spending your time with? What activities do you spend your time doing?

To help give you an idea of what images you might choose, let me walk you through an example:

Jane Doe's dream house would be old fashion architecture, set in the country side, with a large pool. She would have a yellow Lamborghini. Jane Doe imagines herself as a New York Time's best-selling author, and spends her free time reading and knitting. Jane Doe see's herself spending the majority of her time with her husband a daughter. Jane Doe imagines vacationing in Bora Bora and France. Her bank statement show's she has over $100,000 in savings.

So, Jane Doe will find images to support all her desires. These images will make her excited when she sees them, and help her focus on manifesting them into her life. There's many different ways you can represent what you want to manifest, they key is that when you see them they resonate with you and get you all fired up!

Jane Doe could find an image of a $100,000 bill, or print off a bank statement and white out its current numbers and write in $100,000 to represent her savings. Jane Doe can find countless beautiful homes, and home interior photos of what she wants her dream home to look like. She can find in her family photos one of her favorite memories of the family together. She can find pictures of Bora Bora and France that resonate with her; the thing is, it's all up to you! Which images make you go, "I want that!" Use those ones!

It's time to find your images, and start creating your Vision Board collage!

TIP: It can be helpful visually to cluster/group together images for each category

Once you've found your images organize them and glue them on your board, or slot them into your digital collage! Really imagine being/doing/having/visiting each image from you collage. As you put each image on your board say, "Thank you!" for that particular thing! Once you've made your board take some time to look it over and imagine each thing coming to fruition!

Hang your board in a prominent place, or if you went digital make sure to get it onto all your home screens so you will see it frequently!

Today's To-Do List:

- First thing in the Morning do your 10 things I'm Grateful For: Make a mental or written list of 10 things you're grateful for, and for each one complete the sentence: *"Thank you, Thank you, Thank you, for _____, because _____"*

- Make a Vision Board

- Say or think your affirmation for your Cosmic Order from Day 4: *"Thank you, thank you, thank you, for _____"*

- Remember to use your daily affirmations

- The Best Thing That Happened Today: Mentally go through your day looking for the best thing that happened to you. Once you've found the best thing, complete this sentence: *"Thank you, Thank you, Thank you, for _____ it was amazing because _____!"*

Day 8: Meditation

Meditation has an incredible array of benefits! Scientifically studied, meditation has been proven to have a profound impact on our bodies. It improves overall health by reducing stress, improving concentration, slowing aging, improved heart health, improved immune system; suffice it to say there's a long list! There was even a study done at one time where they introduced a group of meditators into a city with high crime rates, and the crime rate reduced! Meditation doesn't just impact the person doing it; it's calming effect Is profound!

In a life where we're used to *doing, doing, doing*, meditation teaches us to just *be*. To be aware, to be perceptive, and to be in the moment. It is a treat, and will help you feel better in taking on your day, as it will reduce your stress and anxiety. Meditating in the morning can help you to have a more focused day, and meditating in the evening can help still your thoughts for a better sleep.

For our purposes, we're using meditation to quiet our mind to better hear cues from the Universe. It will bring you a sense of peace and serenity, and help you to be more present in the moment, which will help you be more aware and more grateful! And you'll still experience all the additional benefits!

For today we are simply going to focus on stilling our minds, centering ourselves, and grounding ourselves in the moment. However, as you continue to practice meditation, before beginning, you can ask a question to the Universe, to get guidance. This helps you build your communication and listening for how the Universe sends you opportunities.

You'll want to find a quiet place to sit, where you won't be disturbed, and you want to have a timer. Why is a timer so important? If you say, "Ok, I'm going to meditate for 5 minutes," and you sit, and start to do so, your mind will keep asking how long it's been, and if you're done yet. You want a timer so you can release that need to know; you'll be told it's been 5 minutes once your timer tells you!

THE BREATH

Get comfortable, sit cross legged, with your neck in line with your spine. Sit tall without forcing it; you just don't want to be hunched over here. Put your right hand on your lower abdomen, just below the belly button. Breathe in deeply, and exhale. Did your belly move? For most people, the answer is, "No, it didn't move." Most people breathe into their chest; if you say, "Take a deep breathe," their chest puffs up and out to the sides. Chest breathing tends to consist of quicker, more shallow breathing.

When you breathe into your belly, all the way into your pelvic floor, several things happen. You are activating your Chakra energy centers, you're connecting to your emotions, and you're relinquishing control. Chest breathing is a learned habit, and while over years and years of doing it, it may feel natural, it's forced. Letting go of that is another aspect of coming to just *be*. Belly breathing is also much slower, and offers greater lung capacity, which means you provide more oxygen to your blood.

Close your eyes and focus on your breathing. Don't force it, let go of that control and allow the breath to travel naturally. You don't need to push your belly out, just let the breath fall gently into your abdomen. Focus on the breath coming in through your nose, travelling down through your chest, and sinking down below your belly button. As you imagine this you should find it easier for the breath to fill your belly, and you will notice your stomach begins to raise and lower as you breathe.

If belly breathing is new to you, you may also notice you start to have some feelings crop up. Our Root Chakra is our primal self, our sense of survival, and independence, which can also make it an emotional hot-spot for fear and worry. Chest breathing keeps us up in our mind and logical thoughts, belly breathing connects us to how we feel. If any uncomfortable feelings come up, acknowledge them, and let them go. As you continue to practice belly breathing, you will find comfort in it, and have a greater sense of self, and inner peace.

THE MEDITATION

Open your eyes and set your timer for 5 minutes. Now you can rest your hands on your thighs or knees, and close your eyes. Clear your mind and focus in on your breath. If thoughts come up don't get upset, simply release them with your next exhale. Continue to come back to the stillness and the silence. Refocus in on your breathing. Continue to do this until your timer goes off.

Meditation really is a simple practice; sit down, and clear your mind. But it can feel challenging, in our busy lives our minds are going 100 miles a minute and to sit in a silence can make us feel antsy. It does get easier with practice, and the thoughts that creep into your mind are normal. Even the most experienced meditator will have to release bubbling thoughts, it is simply part of the process.

Today's To-Do List:

- First thing in the Morning do your 10 things I'm Grateful For: Make a mental or written list of 10 things you're grateful for, and for each one complete the sentence: *"Thank you, Thank you, Thank you, for _____, because _____"*

- Meditate for 5 Minutes

- Say or think your affirmation for your Cosmic Order from Day 4: *"Thank you, thank you, thank you, for _____"*

- Remember to use your daily affirmations

- The Best Thing That Happened Today: Mentally go through your day looking for the best thing that happened to you. Once you've found the best thing, complete this sentence: *"Thank you, Thank you, Thank you, for _____ it was amazing because _____!"*

Day 9: I Love You

The 'I Love You' practice today is all about appreciating, being grateful for, and loving everything you are. Self-love and acceptance is often something we struggle with. As we grow up, and are pushed to grow and learn, as we stumble and struggle, it can make us feel inadequate. We can feel as if we never live up to expectation, no matter how hard we try.

It is through the struggle that we grow; through failure that we learn. We take away much more from failure than we do from success; where we succeed we often haven't learned anything. It is through failure that we flourish IF we do not give up.

FOSTER YOUR NATURAL STRENGTHS

Your strengths are another's weakness, making you unique and special in your own way! We often hear throughout life that anything worth doing is hard, and while overcoming obstacles is a form of growth, this statement also perpetuates a belief that 'If it's easy it's not worthwhile.' So, as a firmly rooted belief, that means we are constantly trying to do things in life that we find very challenging.

We all have different strengths and weaknesses, and we commonly think if it's easy for us, that it's easy for everyone, and therefor dismiss our own strengths. This simply isn't true, if you are good at something, that is what you should dive into! Explore it, go as far as you can go with it! That is unique to you! What we naturally are good at we tend to find great joy in, we have fun watching it come together, and that inner happiness makes life a treat!

Statistically, the thing you thrive at naturally, only about one out of 10,000 people are good at. Imagine if you foster that strength, keep working in that area, and grow it into mastery; then you'd very likely be 1 in 100,000 with that skill! Then that skill, shared with the world, can make a monumental impact!

WHAT ARE YOUR NATURAL SKILLS?

Grab a piece of paper and brainstorm, "What am I good at?" Write down things you tend to do naturally with ease that also make you happy. Maybe you have a keen eye for design, or have a gift with words, or a knack with numbers; whatever it is jog it down. Think about how unique that skill is! It doesn't take much to see that others struggle in that area!

Once you've written out your strengths say, "Thank you, thank you, thank you, for how easy it is for me to do _____!" and make a declaration to yourself, a promise, to develop that skill, "I, _____, hereby promise that I will spend _____ daily focused on developing _____. I realize that while I find this easy, many don't, and it is my duty to share this strength of mine with the world!"

TIME FOR YOURSELF

It's not uncommon for most of us to spend all our time taking care of others, and leaving ourselves last. This must take a full 180 turn; YOU must come first! This is a very challenging concept for many who are used to putting themselves and their needs last. You might feel discomfort at the thought; it's OK this is a process.

When you ride on an airplane, before takeoff the flight attendant walks everyone through the safety procedures in case of an emergency. During that, they explain that when the oxygen masks drop down it's imperative you place your own mask on yourself *before* helping anyone else with theirs. They stress this point because most people would help someone else with their mask before putting on their own mask; it is human nature for us to want to help and nurture others.

If you attempt to help someone with their oxygen mask before yourself, you may end up passing out, not only putting yourself in danger, but having not helped the other person who may need it. When you help yourself first, and put your needs first, you are better able to help everyone else, because you are taken care of. You are stronger, and more resilient, when you come first. This DOES NOT mean you love anyone any less, it just means you love yourself just as much!

You've heard the saying, "If you don't love yourself, how can anybody else?" This couldn't be any truer! The Law of Attraction teaches us that our thoughts must manifest, so if you feel *unworthy*, or *unlovable*, you're going to make that true! When you love yourself, you invite more love into your life!

"Wherever you go, there you are," I love this quote, and it's particularly important to consider when you're working on manifesting the life of your dreams! No matter what you bring into your life, the dream career, dream house, dream romance, etc. YOU will be there, at the center of it all. You need to love that person for who they are! All the external things won't mean a thing if you're not head of heels in love with you!

"10 THINGS I LOVE ABOUT ME"

It's time to work on that self-love! So, grab that piece of paper again, and write out the numbers 1 – 10. Next to each one you're going to complete writing these sentences below with 10 things you love about you! This is a celebration of who you are, how amazing you are, and how unique you are! Love every bit of who you are; this process is going to make you think about all of the incredible things about you!

You can use all of these sentence structures or just one, whatever feels right:

"I love _____ about me!", or, "I'm great at _____ and I love me for that!", or "I'm grateful about

_____ that I do/am!" or, "I love my

_____!"

OH, MY HEART!

This is a very simply, yet very impactful practice of self-love. You can do this at any time, and you can't do it too much! Place your left hand over your heart, and your right hand on top of your left. Close your eyes, and say, or think, "I love you, I love you, I love you!" This is simple affirmation of self-love should instantly lift your spirits and make you feel accepted and cherished. Practice it often!

Today's To-Do List:

- First thing in the Morning do your 10 things I'm Grateful For: Make a mental or written list of 10 things you're grateful for, and for each one complete the sentence: *"Thank you, Thank you, Thank you, for _____, because _____"*
- *Brainstorm your Natural Skills*
- *Make your "10 Things I Love About Me!" list*
- *Do the "Oh, My Heart" Affirmation*
- Say or think your affirmation for your Cosmic Order from Day 4: *"Thank you, thank you, thank you, for _____"*
- Remember to use your daily affirmations
- The Best Thing That Happened Today: Mentally go through your day looking for the best thing that happened to you. Once you've found the best thing, complete this sentence: *"Thank you, Thank you, Thank you, for _____ it was amazing because _____!"*

Day 10: Shift Your Mindset

Today we're going to be going over some concepts to help expand your mind; to continue to look at the world with new perspectives that will help you solidify your Law of Attraction mindset. These concepts are empowering, and will also serve to replace those old belief systems. Remember, as with anything new, it will take time and practice to integrate these into your daily life; continue with gentle reminders to let the old go and welcome the new.

FULL RESPONSIBILITY

This is one of the most challenging aspects of our mindset to shift; and yet once we do it's the most empowering! Taking full responsibility for everything we do, are, and see, and leaving our old blame game habits behind, can prove difficult. It's especially difficult if someone has done something to upset you, but in those times of challenge it's even more important to turn within yourself.

You're manifesting your reality at all times, challenges and all, so it's important when something negative happens that we're aware, on some level, we brought it into our lives. Be it a life lesson, something the

Universe is trying to teach us, or a negative attitude manifesting in some way, we are the source. When we take responsibility, we give ourselves the ability to change at any moment, to improve the future.

Let's say, for instance, you're struggling with finances. It's very easy, and very common, for us to blame money issues on everything and everyone, "Of course I'm broke, my boss pays me squat!" or, "The economy is bad, *that's* why my business is tanking!" or, "The government eats up my paycheck with taxes, no wonder I'm in debt!" The list can go on and on; but the root of the issue is you! You're manifesting your reality at all times, and as soon as you decide to take responsibility for it, the sooner you can change the story! You're in the driver's seat, so don't just slam your foot down on the gas pedal and hope for the best, take the damn wheel and steer where you want to go!

When a negative situation crops up ask yourself, "What could I have done differently?" Begin to reflect on how events unfolded. Where was your mind before these things happened? Were you dwelling on something negative? Were doubts and fears about what you were doing at the back of your mind? Start to be aware of your mindset throughout the day, and review what your thoughts were before a negative situation arouse.

ALIGNMENT

With the Law of Attraction, alignment is an often-discussed aspect of manifestation. In this context it's about being energetically aligned with what we want, in order to be able to manifest it. This sometimes becomes another source of doubt, "Oh, maybe I didn't manifest _____ yet because I'm not in alignment..." Stop. Right. There! We have enough doubt and fear weighing us down for one lifetime without adding in more!

Being in alignment is simply about knowing what you want, and why you want it. It is about feeling good and happy when you think about that thing coming to fruition in your life. All you need to be in alignment is to listen to that intuitive voice within and ask, "Does this *feel* right? Will this make me happy?" If thinking about it makes you feel elated and excited, and warms your heart, you're in alignment!

Now in the instance you don't feel happy, dive into why you thought you wanted it. Why are you feeling doubtful, fearful, or uninspired about manifesting that thing into your life? Were you trying to manifest someone else's dream they had for you? Perhaps how your parents envisioned your life to be? Get clear about why you want what you want!

Being in alignment also means coming from a place of positivity rather than trying to eliminate a negative. For example, if you're trying to manifest $2000 to pay off your credit card debt, you don't want to be focusing on how bad credit card makes you feel. You want to focus on how it feels to be debt free; light and unencumbered. Imagine signing that check, or online banking and hitting the send button to pay that money. Also, imagine all the things you got for that money, in advance of having the pay for them! *Thank you for lending institutions!* Your perspective matters in keeping you in alignment.

BOTH; NOT 'EITHER,' 'OR'

Abundance mindset means we need to realize we can have it all! You can have a bountiful savings account AND your dream home! You can have cake AND your dream body! You can have a vacation AND have time to get caught up on work! Time with your family AND a fulfilling career!

Growing up we're often told about how we have to pick and choose what we want; that we can't have it all! That is a load of BALONEY! When you start to ask yourself, "how can I have both?" your mind will begin to look for new ways to make things happen, and the Universe will be able to show you new paths to take. All you need to do is realize it's possible to have both. The next time you're faced with an 'either, or' situation, ask yourself how you can have both, and let the creative process start!

THIS OR SOMETHING BETTER!

As we know from our previous lessons, the Universe can see much more than we can see. We've been working on our faith muscle to be patient and trusting that the Universe will guide us down the right path, to manifest what we desire. The next step is trusting that it can bring us to things even BETTER than what we imagined we wanted! When you give the Universe room to work its magic, boy oh boy, can it surprise you in the best possible ways!

Grab out you Top 10 Manifestation List and you're going to read through the list, giving gratitude for each one, and give the Universe room to surprise you, "Thank you, thank you, Thank you for _____ or something better!" I get *really* excited when I add 'or something better' to the end of my desires, because I begin to think about how I might get surprised with something incredible! It's like waiting for Christmas morning and getting the most wonderous gift from someone who loves you dearly!

Today's To-Do List:

- First thing in the Morning do your 10 things I'm
  Grateful For: Make a mental or written list of 10
  things you're grateful for, and for each one complete
  the sentence: *"Thank you, Thank you, Thank you, for*
  _____, *because* _____ *"*

- Be aware of your thoughts, and if you find yourself
  blaming something or someone for your situation,
  stop, and ask yourself what preceded that event in
  your mind.

- If an Either/Or situation presents itself today, ask
  yourself "How can I have both?"

- Use gratitude for your Top 10 Manifestation List,
  "Thank you, thank you, Thank you for
  _____ *or something*
  better!"

- Say or think your affirmation for your Cosmic Order
  from Day 4: *"Thank you, thank you, thank you, for*
  _____ *"*

- Remember to use your daily affirmations

- The Best Thing That Happened Today: Mentally go
  through your day looking for the best thing that

happened to you. Once you've found the best thing, complete this sentence: *"Thank you, Thank you, Thank you, for _____ it was amazing because _____!"*

Day 11: Forgiveness

Holding onto anger and resentment towards someone hurts us more than it will ever hurt them. I mean, do they even realize you're angry? Sometimes in life people wrong us in certain ways, sometimes big or small, and sometimes life-changing monumental ways. Forgiveness isn't about them, it's about you; liberating yourself from giving them space in your thoughts.

"HOLDING ON TO ANGER IS LIKE GRASPING A HOT COAL WITH THE INTENT OF THROWING IT AT SOMEONE ELSE; YOU ARE THE ONE WHO GETS BURNED."

— BUDDHA

No thought lives in your head rent free; so, if negative thoughts are dwelling there it's time to evict them! It's important to know that that this practice has nothing to do with whose right, or whose wrong; it's all about releasing the past! You cannot fully live in the present moment if your mind is still mulling over a past situation again and again.

If you're in the middle of a difficult situation with another person, this exercise may feel particularly challenging. But it can also be profoundly powerful; when you release that negative energy and instead invite the good, opportunities arise to solve those difficulties in a more amicable way. Keep reminding yourself that releasing anger is about freeing up your own mental space.

10 GOOD THINGS ABOUT THIS

It can feel most challenging to find things to be grateful for about a situation you're not happy about, but it also makes it that much more powerful! If you can find the good within the worst experiences, you will start attracting the best things into your world. Ask yourself these questions to help find your 10 things to be grateful for:

- What did I learn from this situation?
- Were there good aspects about this situation before it turned sour?
- What did I like about that person originally?
- Did knowing this person bring someone else into my life that I'm grateful for?

- Putting their shoes on, can I understand (not necessarily agree with) where that person is coming from?
- What positive things came out of this situation?
- How did knowing this person help me grow as a human being?

Usually, before a negative situation with someone occurs, we know them in a positive or neutral way. Let's say, for example, you've had a falling out with a once good friend. Before that happened, you had good times together, you connected on a deeper level, and those wonderful aspects are no less true now. Be grateful for those times, even though they've passed. Perhaps through them you met your current partner, or a current close friend, who you would otherwise not have met. Sometimes people come and go out of our life as a conduit for us to meet the people we need to.

Find one relationship where you're currently holding onto anger and resentment, it doesn't matter how old or fresh the incident is, what the person did, if it's a business relationship, or a personal one; if you still get work up thinking about it then that's the one you're going to be working through.

Either write down, or mentally make your list of 10 things to be grateful for about that situation or person. The more understanding you have from taking a broader perspective, the easier time you'll have finding things to be grateful for. After you have your 10, say, "Thank you for the lesson's learned."

I RELEASE THIS

Next, it's time to forgive; to lift the burden of carrying that heavy baggage called resentment, and liberate yourself. Say, or think, "_____, I forgive you for _____. I choose to no longer dwell on this, to free myself from the weight of resentment. I choose to live fully in the present. I choose to be happy!"

This simply act of forgiving can make you feel as if you've had 50 pounds lifted off your chest! If you've been holding onto a grudge with more than one person, you can use this practice on each one until you're completely liberated.

Today's To-Do List:

- First thing in the Morning do your 10 things I'm Grateful For: Make a mental or written list of 10 things you're grateful for, and for each one complete the sentence: *"Thank you, Thank you, Thank you, for _____, because _____"*

- Find 10 things that are Good about the negative situation

- Forgive the person you're holding onto anger with

- Say or think your affirmation for your Cosmic Order from Day 4: *"Thank you, thank you, thank you, for _____"*

- Remember to use your daily affirmations

- The Best Thing That Happened Today: Mentally go through your day looking for the best thing that happened to you. Once you've found the best thing, complete this sentence: *"Thank you, Thank you, Thank you, for _____ it was amazing because _____!"*

Day 12: Money

Money, the hot topic! Oh, the mixed feeling we have about money! We love it, we hate it, we need it, we resent it; it's a wonder it shows up in our lives at all with the push and pull nature of our feelings towards it!

When it comes to money, the first thing we must do is de-criminalize it. I mean, it's not like money broke into your house, kicked your dog, punched you in the face, and robbed you! Let's get some perspective on these mixed feelings we have about money.

This is going to go all the way back to our beliefs; those deep-rooted connections we made to money in our formative years. We weren't born with an opinion on money, we learned about it from those around us; parents, guardians, teachers, society, etc. behaviors and attitudes towards money are learned. Think about it, how many of these statements have you heard your whole life, and possibly, have even said or thought yourself:

- Money is the root of all evil
- Money doesn't grow on trees
- Rich people are greedy

- There's never enough money

- The best things in life are free

- Money isn't that important

- It's better to give than to receive

- It's harder to get rich these days

- It's selfish to have so much, when others have so
  little

The more we hear something in life, the easier it is to believe it as true. These common sayings are rampant in our society; the strife and struggles people have felt with money has caused a lot of anger, grief, and jealousy that's lead to some negative thoughts about money. It becomes easier for people to dismiss money as unimportant, or to compare it to something that has nothing to do with money, in an attempt to make money seem less important.

For example, often people will say, "Time with friends and family is more important than money," umm, what does one have to do with the other? How about time with friends and family is important AND money is important! And let's take it a step further; if you are financially free, you can fully enjoy that time with friends and family instead of worrying about all your bills and debt while you're with your loved ones! Remember our 'either/or' training we did? You can have BOTH!

Worried money will corrupt you? Lay that fear to rest. Money will only help you to be more of who you already are; it's like life's free pass to follow your heart! If you're naturally a very thoughtful, kind, giving human being, money will allow you to be more of that on a bigger scale. Naturally an A-hole? It'll let you do more of that too. It's the very few rich jerks who make headlines that make everyone think money corrupts, but those people would be doing crappy things even if they were broke; don't fool yourself into thinking money made them that way!

Does having a lot of money make you feel guilty about all those living with less? STOP. RIGHT. THERE! How does YOU being broke help anyone else? It doesn't. In fact, if you have more money you have the ability to help those in need. It's also important to remember, there isn't a finite amount of money, so it's not like one person can horde it and others then have to go without; they just keep printing more and more money by the day. It's a growing, not a diminishing, resource.

WHAT IS MONEY?

So, let's gain some clarity here. What is money? Money is energy. That's it! Long, long, ago, we used to trade services to get what we needed. Some guy built your fence, you gave him one of your livestock in exchange. We now, rarely, work in exchange for services or goods, so money is a symbol of exchange, a glorified I.O.U. that you can cash in anywhere!

HOW YOU TRULY FEEL

So, how do you *really* feel about money? You might think you've got a good relationship with money, but most of us are very conflicted in how we feel about it. Grab a pen and a piece of paper; you're going to write a love letter to money to tell money how you feel about it! A heart to heart, hold nothing back, lay all the cards on the table, kinda letter!

EXAMPLE

Dear money,

I wish you came around more often. I feel like I never have enough of you, like I'm always just waiting for you to show up. I hate it. And you go as fast as you come. I feel terrified you're never going to come back after you leave, and it ruins all my free time. I wish you'd just come and stay!

I don't feel like I can trust you. I'm scared when I have you that I'm going to lose you. I don't know what to do with you, or how to make enough of you to feel secure. I feel like I'm always at your mercy. I'm so happy when you show up and I'm furious when you go. Can't you just stay put?

I want to have enough of you to feel happy. I want to stop worrying about you. I want to enjoy our time together and I don't want that time to end.

Sincerely, John Doe

P.S. please come back soon!

This exercise gives us some clear insights into what's really going on beneath the surface. If you notice you have these push-and-pull feelings around money, don't get frustrated, most people feel similarly. This is just for you to recognize those feelings, so you can begin to release those fears. Come back to this exercise once a month to see how your feelings are changing as your view on money changes.

I LOVE MONEY

We're inundated with negative money sayings; and as we know the more we hear something the more we believe it! So, we are going to create our own new money sayings! It is time to fall in love with money! Money is the conduit to do and be all the things you want in life! Let's celebrate what we love about money! Grab a pen and a piece of paper, and make a list of 10 things you love about money!

MONEY MANIFESTING

Money is a means to an end, so when we think about manifesting money, it's much more emotionally charged when we think about what we're manifesting it for! If you try to manifest a dollar amount for the sake of having the money, it's hard to get all giddy and excited about it, and that means it's hard to feel gratitude for it. But if you decide you want to manifest $5000 for a vacation to Bora Bora, that you can get excited about! You can imagine the time on the beach, the view of the ocean, the time with loved ones. Or maybe you want to manifest $10,000 for a down payment on a house, then start visualizing the home, what you want in that home, how it will feel to live there!

Choose 1-3 things you wish to manifest that require money to obtain. Use the visualization practice from Day 2 for each of these things you wish to manifest. Imagine how good it will feel to pay for each of these things you want. What will you do when you first receive them? Who will you celebrate with? What is the sensory experience you'll go through; touch, taste, smell, hear, and see?

Say for each item, "Thank you, thank you, thank you, for the money to pay for _____! Receiving _____ makes me feel _____ and brings great joy to my life!"

NATURE ABHORS A VACUUM

Ever noticed after you've emptied out a closet, cleared of a table, or emptied out a drawer, it's filled back up in no time? A space is magnetically charged to be filled! I want you to close your eyes and visualize your bank account. Imagine your account as a gigantic receptacle or clear vase. Put a numerical value on what "Full" would be for this gigantic vessel; stretch your mind to reach for a large number just outside of your comfort zone. That might be $5,000, $100,000, $500,000 or $50M; the point is to pick a number that feels big, but attainable, from where you're at now.

Next, I want you to visualize this receptacle filled part way up with your current savings, even if it only a few dollars, imagine them in there! See all of that space in that receptacle to be filled up! Imagine money flowing into it effortlessly, and it is filling up to the top. When you mentally see yourself with room to grow with your finances, you create the vacuum effect. Give the Universe the space you need for that money to appear!

Today's To-Do List:

- First thing in the Morning do your 10 things I'm Grateful For: Make a mental or written list of 10 things you're grateful for, and for each one complete the sentence: *"Thank you, Thank you, Thank you, for _____, because _____"*
- *Write a Love Letter to money*
- Write out 10 things you Love About Money
- Visualize what you want to manifest money for
- Visualize your bank account using the receptacle/vase practice
- Use the money Affirmations from day 3
- Say or think your affirmation for your Cosmic Order from Day 4: *"Thank you, thank you, thank you, for _____"*
- Remember to use your daily affirmations
- The Best Thing That Happened Today: Mentally go through your day looking for the best thing that happened to you. Once you've found the best thing, complete this sentence: *"Thank you, Thank you, Thank you, for _____ it was amazing because _____!"*

Manifesting Reminder!

Pay attention to nudges from the Universe to take action; don't try to analyze or figure out why you feel the urge to do something, just follow it. The 'how' is the domain of the Universe.

Day 13: Relationships

Our connections and experiences with other people create deep meaning in our lives. We are inspired to do great things for others, and an experience is so much more enjoyable when we can share it with someone else, communicating thoughts and ideas; it's the relationships we form that help us experience life fully. We are helped by others, and we help people too. The connections we form throughout our lives often play a huge role in what we do and who we become.

Our animal relationships are just as important. The unspoken bonds we create with other living creatures helps us to view the world in entirely new ways. Our perceptions of life as humans are often dragging our thoughts to looking back at the past, or ahead to the future. Our animal companions help remind us to the live the present moment.

Each encounter helps us grow and experience the world in a new way. Our relationships bring us great joy and help us to grow. Being thankful for relationships ensures we continue to have blossoming relationships full of joy.

THE PEOPLE WHO HELPED US

Think back to a time in your life when you were struggling and someone helped you get through that tough spot. It's as if you had your own personal guardian angel. Perhaps it was a friend, parents, sibling, teacher, or mentor who helped you see past your struggles. Maybe they helped you with kind words, advice, or their calming presence and understanding, or, perhaps they had an involved approach in helping your through your challenges. Regardless of how they helped you, they left you uplifted.

Small encounters and compassionate acts from another human being can change the direction of our lives in a split second. Take a moment to thank someone who profoundly impacted your life, be their act large or small, because it left your changed. It doesn't matter if they are still in your life, or still alive, thank them for how they helped you become the person you are today.

"Thank you _____. When you

_____ it completely changed my life

because

_____

and I am truly grateful."

THE PEOPLE WE LOVE

People come and go from our lives over the years. Think about those currently closest to you; family, friends, co-workers, whom you appreciate spending time with dearly. Think about the people who make you smile, and the fun you have sharing time together. Say, "Thank you _____ for being in my life!" to each person you think of who you are grateful for!

HEALING A BROKEN OR STRAINED RELATIONSHIP

While it can be challenging when we are experiencing a rift in a relationship, the way to heal it is through gratitude. Perhaps you had a falling out with a friend, or have grown apart from a partner, or have always felt strain when trying to get along with a parent; whatever the case may be, to heal that relationship and make it better we must focus on what we want that relationship to be.

If at some point that relationship was a positive one, look for those things that you loved about that person and how your spent your time together. Find 10 things you're grateful for from your past experience with that person. Say, think, or write, "I'm truly grateful for

_____."

If it has always been a rocky relationship, try to look for the good qualities in the other person; everyone has them. Think about the lessons they've helped you learn. If it's a parent, think about what sacrifices they might have made to help you as you've grown. Say, think, or write, "Thank you, thank you, thank you, for helping me

_____." OR, "I Appreciate

_____ about you."

If you're having a very difficult time with these, you may also wish to revisit Day 11: Forgiveness practice.

THE PEOPLE WE'VE YET TO MEET

Life has countless opportunities for us to make new connections with people; so often unplanned! Someone you meet at a grocery store, a friend of a friend at a gathering, a new employee at a favorite hangout; the opportunities are limitless. Invite the Universe to line you up with a new kindred spirit with which to share this life with! "Thank you, thank you, thank you, for the new friendship!"

OUR FURRY FRIENDS

You may or may not have animals directly in your life. If you do have pets, take a moment today to go and lay with them and share a moment. Animals live in the moment, they act from their hearts, and teach us to be much more present. They can fill us with incredible joy.

If you do not live with animals, and are able too, take a walk in the park and observe birds, squirrels, chipmunks and any other wild life that happens to show up. If that's not a possibility, pull up some videos online of animals, and observe how the live in the now.

Remind yourself to live in the present moment. If you find yourself dwelling on the past, or thinking about the future today, breathe deeply, and come back to this moment. Sense your surroundings, recognize what's happening right now, and be in that moment.

Today's To-Do List:

- First thing in the Morning do your 10 things I'm Grateful For: Make a mental or written list of 10 things you're grateful for, and for each one complete the sentence: *"Thank you, Thank you, Thank you, for* _____, *because* _____ *"*

- Complete The People we Love, The People who helped us, Healing a broken Relationship, The People we've yet to meet, and Our Furry Friends practices

- Say or think your affirmation for your Cosmic Order from Day 4: *"Thank you, thank you, thank you, for* _____ *"*

- Remember to use your daily affirmations

- The Best Thing That Happened Today: Mentally go through your day looking for the best thing that happened to you. Once you've found the best thing, complete this sentence: *"Thank you, Thank you, Thank you, for* _____ *it was amazing because* _____ *!"*

AMANDA ROSE

Day 14: Travel & Experience

Let me start off by saying that not EVERYONE wants to travel, and that's perfectly alright! If you are doing this practice and have no inclination to travel, you'll be using this as a means to attract the new experiences you want into your life. Traveling is a way for us to learn and grow, to broaden our perspective, experience new climates, cultures, and ways of life. New experiences can be found all around us however, within our own communities, so if you don't wish to travel, focus on those experiences that would enrich your life near to home.

Now, if you DO have a desire to travel but don't see how, for whatever reason, time constraints, finances, career, etc. then you should focus on your travel destinations; let the Universe clear the way to make it happen! You can also do both aspects, attracting experiences close to home and abroad! Whatever you desire, we're going to manifest it! I will guide you through these exercises assuming you're focused on both.

WHERE OR WHAT

The first thing you need to do is get clear about where you want to go, or what you want to experience! You can always update your list, so don't worry about trying to write down everything you've ever wanted to do, or everywhere you've ever wanted to visit. Aim to write down 3-5 places/experiences. If you, however, have always dreamed of travelling, or have a long list of things you wish to do, go for it, write them all down!

Try not to censor yourself; you're not trying to book this, you don't have to schedule this; we often try to jump 10 steps ahead when we think about the things we want, and then we will talk ourselves out of them when we can't see a clear path towards making it happen. You are simply letting your imagination and heart's desires have their opportunity to express themselves right now. You're getting clear on what you'd like to experience, nothing beyond the end result should enter your mind!

We can travel for various reasons; vacations, experiences, visiting friends or family who don't live nearby, cultural immersion, relaxation, historic sites, to get to a specific event or place, EXAMPLES: Spa weekend, yoga retreat, vow renewal, concerts, etc. Let your mind run free to think about all the things that make you excited!

Experiential wise, what's something you've always wanted to do? Even if your town is small and doesn't offer much, local cities within driving distance often will, so don't limit yourself by thinking, "Oh, well that's no possible," give yourself permission to explore what excites you! Maybe taking a class at a local college on a subject that interests you, maybe an art class, maybe getting involved with a charity, maybe gardening, rock climbing, museum tours, concerts, learning a new language; the list of possibilities is endless. So, what makes your heart ba-bomb with excitement when you think about it? Write it down!

VISUALIZATION

So, let's say Jane Doe came up with 12 places and things she wants to experience. She's going to take her top 5 and work through visualizing them:

1. Vacation in Cancun, Mexico
2. Visit the pyramids in Egypt
3. A cultural trip to Ireland
4. Taking a pottery class

5. Sky diving

One by one Jane is going to go through her list and visualize what it's like to experience each one. She's not going to worry about accuracy about the things and places she's never been, she's just going to use her imagination to create the experience of being there.

Example Travel Cancun, Mexico, vacation:

Jane Doe imagines stepping off of the plane into the warm Mexican weather, smelling the coconut sea breeze, and how happy she will feel. She imagines the bus pulling up to the hotel to drop her off, and how beautiful the building is. She imagines walking into her room, and how pretty it is, overlooking the ocean. She pictures herself walking along the beach and how good the warm sand feels beneath her feet. She imagines hearing the rustling of the palm trees and the lapping waves from the surf. She imagines swimming in the ocean and seeing tropical fish swim by. She thinks about the delicious authentic Mexican food and eating crispy, salty, tortilla chips with guacamole.

Example Experience, Sky Diving:

Jane doe imagines putting on her gear and getting into the airplane. She imagines how it feels as it makes the steep accent. She feels her heart race with excited anticipation as they climb steeply. She feels the cool air as they get higher altitude. Jane imagines putting on her parachute and having the instructor check it to make sure she's safe. She feels exhilaration as the captain turns on the green light to jump, and the instructor opens hatch. Jane Doe pictures herself securing her googles and walking up to the door. She imagines taking the leap, and how free she'll feel free-falling in the air.

Jane Doe makes the experiences as sensory as possibly to engage her senses. She is only imagining the end result, not how she found the time or the funds to go. Picture the end result you want, and imagine living it and get into as much detail as you can! Do this for each place and experience on your list!

GRATITUDE

After you've visualized experiencing each of the 5 things you've chosen from your list, say thank you as if they've already happened. Give the Universe the ability to work to bring those experiences into your reality!

"Thank you, thank you, thank you, for the amazing trip to

_____!"

or

"Thank you, thank you, thank you, for what I learned doing

_____!"

or

"I'm truly grateful for getting to experience

_____!"

Today's To-Do List:

- First thing in the Morning do your 10 things I'm Grateful For: Make a mental or written list of 10 things you're grateful for, and for each one complete the sentence: *"Thank you, Thank you, Thank you, for _____, because _____"*

- Let your heart tell you what it is you want to experience and write down what places to visit, or things to do, that come to mind

- Use visualization on your top 5 places/things

- Use gratitude to bring your desired experiences into your reality

- Say or think your affirmation for your Cosmic Order from Day 4: *"Thank you, thank you, thank you, for _____"*

- Remember to use your daily affirmations

- The Best Thing That Happened Today: Mentally go through your day looking for the best thing that happened to you. Once you've found the best thing, complete this sentence: *"Thank you, Thank you, Thank you, for _____ it was amazing because _____!"*

Day 15: Career

For many of us, our career or job takes up a massive portion of our waking hours, and in some cases, it takes up the majority. When we spend so much time devoted to our work it's crucial we find joy in our work. Whether or not you're currently working your dream job, the fastest way to attract opportunities to enjoy your work more is to be grateful for your current situation.

Just like all aspects of our lives, how we think and feel about our job affects what we attract to ourselves. If you're constantly complaining, focusing on what you don't like, thinking about the co-workers you dislike, the deadlines that stress you out, etc. your work life will be miserable. You need to focus on what you enjoy, so you are attracting more of those things to you. And look for the good within each situation, whether the situation itself is good or bad, to program you mind to not dwell on the negatives.

We're going to walk through different aspects of working, and how to ask yourself questions that get you to seek out the positives:

EMPLOYED

If you're currently employed, first off, be grateful you have a job! Not everyone does, and it's all too easy to take it for granted. Think about the people you work with, what relationships have you developed that you otherwise wouldn't have made if you hadn't worked this job? Perhaps you don't have common ground with any of your co-workers; think about what that's helped you learn about relationships. What new skills has this job taught you? Not all skills we learn are obvious, sometimes we learn to get better at interpersonal relationships, other times we learn a more tangible skill, but all the things we learn and experience help us to grow.

Be thankful for your paycheck from your employer, that allows you to pay your bills and get what you want in life. Have you received promotions in the past? Thank you for promotions! Think about the job you perform, which aspects do you enjoy the most? Even if we're not doing a job we love, there are aspects of everything we do we can find joy or satisfaction in. When there is a task to do and an option in what part you can play, what do you naturally gravitate to?

SELF-EMPLOYED

Whether you're a contractor, artist, CEO of a large corporation, or a company of 1, it takes courage to take this less travelled path! Thank yourself for being brave. Think about all the liberties that come with being self-employed; you set your own rules, you're the boss, you choose the projects you do and the people you want to work with! You learn all about self-discipline, and self-motivation.

Think about the field you've decided to work in, what drew you to it? Why are you passionate about what you do? Do you thrive on creativity, or the push of a deadline? Perhaps you work from home; be grateful for not having to get stuck in the grid-lock of a daily commute, the extra time with family and pets, and the tax write offs you get.

UNEMPLOYED

If you're currently unemployed, look for the things to be grateful within that. You could be grateful for previous employment opportunities, for the time off it's given you, perhaps you had Unemployment Insurance that's carried you through the interim, or had the opportunity to study a new skill set. Perhaps being unemployed has given you the freedom you needed to pursue getting your own business started, or time to work on a long overdue project;

whatever the case may be look for the blessings within your situation.

PASSIVE INCOME & TEMPORARY PROJECTS

Perhaps you work partially, or fully, on projects to build passive income streams, or lump sum income. Think about how unique the work you do is, and what attracts you to working on these projects. Perhaps you write books or articles, or create online courses, or run seminars, or run a Multi-Level Marketing business, or do public speaking engagements; whatever it is, these tend to be driven by deep rooted passion. These projects often require a great deal of work up-front, without pay until the project is either up and running, or completed.

Think about what inspired you to do what you're doing; what motivated you do get started? What about your project or passive income model excited you? How will what you're doing change the lives of the people it touches? How will it affect your life once the project is in full swing? Enjoying the journey is much easier when you see a clear destination for these projects; knowing your efforts are for a greater purpose!

DREAM JOB

If you're already working your dream job, take some time to acknowledge that, and to be thankful for at least 10 things about it. If you're not yet working your dream job, now is the time to visualize it. Do you know what your dream job is? If not, take some time to think this over. One of the easiest ways to help determine what would bring you great joy is to go through this exercise:

If you had $10 Billion dollars, no restrictions and no limitations, what would you do? After the vacations, the fun purchases, the new house and car, how would you spend your time? What would your days look like? What are you naturally drawn to do? Maybe you envision yourself gardening, or doing yoga, journaling, playing music, cooking, partying, studying a new subject, reading, working on cars; the list of possibilities is endless, the key is that it excites YOU and you'd naturally do that, given you had the money and time to do so.

Whatever you saw yourself doing, that activity (or activities), can be monetized; there's a job in that field OR an ability to create one. We often feel because we enjoy doing something, or because it comes easy for us, that there's no way that we could make money doing it; work is work and play is play. This is just another belief we need to uproot from our subconscious. Your work can fill you with joy and passion, and make you want to leap out of bed each day in anticipated excitement of what is to come!

There are endless ways to turn your naturally inclined activities into your dream job! Let's take reading for example; you might find yourself inclined to work at a library, or as a proof reader, an editor, or it may inspire you to write your own book, to name a few. With mighty google at our side, it can help us see the possibilities! Not sure what your favorite activity could translate to as a career? Try googling "Jobs that involve _____" to see what pops up. It may also be an opportunity for you to create your own business!

GUIDANCE

If you're still not entirely clear on what your dream job will be, ask the Universe for guidance. You can do this by asking, "What is my dream job?" before meditating, and see what ideas and images are presented to you. If you think you have an idea of what you'd like to do, you can ask, "Should I pursue _____?" with a pendulum, or, ask the Universe to show you a sign to indicate. A sign could be a number, an animal, or some meaningful symbol to you.

VISUALIZATION

Once you're clear on your dream job, find a quiet place to sit where you won't be interrupted and you're going to mentally walk through a day living that. When will your day begin? What will you wear? Where will you work? What will you be working on? How do you feel working on the daily tasks? Do you work with others, or alone? Imagine what your work space looks like. How is what you're doing making an impact? What do you see and hear? Do you have an office, and if yes, what does it look like? Get into as much detail as possible, and for each thing say, "Thank you!" as you imagine living it.

Today's To-Do List:

- First thing in the Morning do your 10 things I'm Grateful For: Make a mental or written list of 10 things you're grateful for, and for each one complete the sentence: *"Thank you, Thank you, Thank you, for* _____, *because* _____ "

- Be grateful for your current work situation

- Focus on determining your dream job OR if you are already doing your dream job, then focus on being grateful for 10 things about your dream job

- Visualize a day in the life of your dream job and be grateful as if you're already living it

- Say or think your affirmation for your Cosmic Order from Day 4: *"Thank you, thank you, thank you, for* _____ "

- Remember to use your daily affirmations

- The Best Thing That Happened Today: Mentally go through your day looking for the best thing that happened to you. Once you've found the best thing, complete this sentence: *"Thank you, Thank you, Thank you, for* _____ *it was amazing because* _____ !"

Day 16: Love & Romance

We all, at our core, seek to love and be loved. We wish to share our life experiences, and express affection. Sometimes love can come in and out of our lives frequently, and sometimes we have a long time to nurture a long-lasting romance. Whether you're in a relationship, seeking one, or enjoying some time being solo, we're going to spend some time today celebrating romantic love!

What we focus on expands, so taking time to appreciate a current relationship you'll help it deepen. If you're seeking love, visualization it and working on your faith in the Universe, will help the Universe to connect you to your ideal partner. If you're enjoying alone time, and not seeking companionship at this time, take some time to find the freedom and joys within that to fill you with happiness in your days.

IN A ROMANTIC RELATIONSHIP

When you're in a romantic relationship, there are a lot of wonderful times to celebrate. When you first fall in love, there's a sense of joy a euphoria about all aspects of life. We tend to feel our problems melt away and just focus in on our new-found love. This blissful time when new love blossoms is captivating; a special time to remember. Think back to when you first met your partner and began your relationship together. Remember the discoveries you had as you learned about them, and shared about yourself. Where did you spend your time together? What special moments stand out to you? As you recall each special moment, place your hand over your heart and say, "Thank you!"

As a relationship progresses, and the euphoria wears off, we begin to balance life out again with spending time with our partner. Some people confuse this time with 'falling out of love' because that initial 'high' we feel is gone; but this is really where love begins to deepen. You're beginning to know your partner intimately, their hopes, desires, bad habits, and good ones. The rose-colored glasses have come off, and this is the point where you see you love them for who they are, and they love you for who you are. You become comfortable around each other and are able to drop any pretense. Close your eyes and picture your partner, and say, "I love you just the way you are!"

Think about any major life events you've shared together. If you and your partner are married, close your eyes and remember that day; revisit your steps throughout that day and remember all the magical moments. Perhaps you and your partner have travelled, been to large family events, adopted pets, or had children together; think through the many things you've shared throughout your time together. Put your hand on your heart and say, "Thank you for all of the magical moments I've shared with

_____!"

If your relationship is new, think to the events you have to look forward to. Imagine the things you'd like to do and share with your partner. Get as detailed as possible, and get excited about it! If your long-time partner has passed away, remember all the incredible times you've had together. Know that the love you had will always be cherished in your heart, and that we are all beings of energy, and therefore we are never really separated.

SEEKING A ROMANTIC RELATIONSHIP

If you're currently looking for love in your life, you have an exciting adventure ahead! It's important as we focus on manifesting a romantic relationship in our lives that we do not try to force a relationship with a single individual in mind, and that we let go of any neediness. As with all manifesting, we need to trust and have faith in the process.

There are more than enough negative social views on finding a relationship from our mid-twenties onward. Read through the following sayings and see if any of them stick out as 'true' to you, or if you find yourself saying or thinking them:

- There aren't any single people where I live
- I already had my one shot at love
- All the good ones are taken
- Dating takes too much time and effort
- The people I meet are always awful
- I'm too old to find anyone
- I'll never find the right one

If these, or anything similar, have crept into your mind, it's time to uproot them! Love comes in all sizes, shapes, and ages; life takes us all in different directions and with billions and billions of people on this earth, you're lying to yourself if you think you'll never find anyone. Trust that there's someone out there (in fact many someone's) who could kindle the flame in your heart.

Replace those negative sayings with positive affirmations:

"I love dating!"

"There are incredible people out there!"

"Love knows no bounds!"

"I will find the right person!"

The most important thing you can do is get clear about the kind of person you'd like to attract. What qualities do they have? What activities do you want to share with them? Do you want to have a family together? Get married? Travel? Picture it all in vivid detail.

Make room for them to come into your life! The Universe responds to belief and action; so, show the Universe that you are serious about bringing someone into your life! Clear space in your closet for their things, set up a night table for them on the other side of the bed (if you're on a small bed, buy a bigger one!). Clear out some space in any storage space you have, to be able to share it with them.

Start cooking nice meals; all too often when we're living alone we get lazy about our food when we're cooking 'just for us'. By making nice meals for yourself you're, 1. Loving yourself more! And, 2. Preparing to share delicious meals and experiences with your new love. Food is a conduit we use to share our love and nurturing, so start getting in the mood now!

You've heard the old adage, "Dress for Success," and that applies to attracting a new mate too! No, I'm not saying to dress like somebody else, or what you *think* your prospective partner is looking for. But dress in a way that makes you feel confident, and sexy, and empowered, and that's 100% you. After all, if you're looking for a long-term relationship you do not want to pretend to be something you're not, but let's face it, after we've been living by ourselves for a while it gets easier and easier to leave the house with un-brushed hair and sweat pants with a tear in them. Be authentically you, and be presentable.

Listen to that inner nudge; when you're visualizing your prospective mate, and lining up your life to receive them, your signal is telling the Universe, "I'm ready!" So, now, it's your turn to listen for the Universe communicating to you about what you need to do. You may very well meet your prospective mate on a regular outing to the grocery store, at a work meeting, or any variety of your regular spots. However, you might not, and you may be nudged to do something to line yourself up to be able to meet them. Maybe you'll have an impulse to buy a concert ticket, visit a comedy club, or sign up for a class or charity run; if the impulse comes, don't question it, just go with it! Test that faith muscle and trust the Universe is bringing you together.

NOT SEEKING A ROMANTIC RELATIONSHIP

There are times in our lives where we're perfectly content to have time to ourselves; to indulge our own passions. Recognizing this time as a gift to rediscover ourselves is so important. We do not need another person to complete our lives. You are enough. Think about the things you want to pursue that being on your own grants you the time for. Self-care, self-growth, and defining who you are, can most easily come about during these times. Be grateful for the solitude.

Our relationships are wonderful, they bring us incredible joy, but it's fair to say that they do take a lot of our time to nurture. When we have this time to ourselves, it allows us to do things we otherwise didn't make the time for while being in a relationship. This can be a magnificently creative time. Brainstorm the things you'd like to do while you're on your own.

Today's To-Do List:

- First thing in the Morning do your 10 things I'm Grateful For: Make a mental or written list of 10 things you're grateful for, and for each one complete the sentence: *"Thank you, Thank you, Thank you, for _____, because _____"*

- Be grateful for your current situation in romance, be thankful for past experiences, and be thankful for what is to come

- Say or think your affirmation for your Cosmic Order from Day 4: *"Thank you, thank you, thank you, for _____"*

- Remember to use your daily affirmations

- The Best Thing That Happened Today: Mentally go through your day looking for the best thing that happened to you. Once you've found the best thing, complete this sentence: *"Thank you, Thank you, Thank you, for _____ it was amazing because _____!"*

Day 17: Success

Success; this concept of achievement has us strive to do our best, or leaves us feeling like we never measure up. But what does success REALLY mean? The Dictionary defines it as:

noun

1.

the favorable or prosperous termination of attempts or end eavors; the accomplishment of one's goals.

2.

the attainment of wealth, position, honors, or the like.

3.

a performance or achievement that is marked by success, as by the attainment of honors:

The play was an instant success.

4.

a person or thing that has had success, as measured by a ttainment of goals, wealth, etc.:

She was a great success on the talk show.

5.

Obsolete. outcome.

What is most interesting about Success, is that it is in reference to the end results of a pursuit; in relativity to the actions needed to achieve success, this final triumph is but a fraction of a fraction of the time involved. It's no wonder most people feel inadequate when striving for success; it's a brief and fleeting moment at the end of a long haul.

As we discuss success today, we need to redefine what it means to us individually. If the journey is the main part of our experience, how can we find the joy in that? What are the triumphs along the way? Yes, we're working towards one big finale, but, that's just one moment in a long journey. What are those amazing things that are happening along the way to add up to that big win?

Success is often equated to money or work, but it's in no way limited to that! You can find success in relationships, raising your children, training a pet, any hobby, education; in anything you choose to do! You also have to decide what metrics bring you the greatest joy when determining how you track your success.

SUCCESS METRICS

Let's say your goal is to earn an additional $100,000 this year, and you're embarking on a new business venture to earn it. In our previous lesson with money, we know money in and of itself is just a conduit to something else; meaning focusing on the money alone won't bring much joy in your metrics tracking. It may also bring you a great deal of frustration if you focus on tracking the money at first; pending on your business model you may not be seeing monetary gains for quite some time, which will leave you feeling like you're at a complete stand still even if you're doing everything right.

But let's say, same circumstances, and you choose to monitor your success by how many new customers are signing up for your product or service. That's a trackable metric which will be growing at a rapid pace. This gives you something meaningful to watch, knowing each person signing up is having their life positively impacted by what you have to offer. This is going to make you feel good for making an impact in peoples' lives, and the end result is moving you closer to your monetary goal as well. You can now celebrate the milestones of customer growth leading up to your goal!

WHAT DOES SUCCESS MEAN TO YOU?

The most important thing for you to determine is what success means to you! As you've discovered throughout this course, everything stems from your belief system. So, the question is, are you creating success based on what you want, or based on previous notions you picked up about what success "should be"? Often a parent or guardian had certain world views or aspirations for you, you could be intentionally trying to use those as your guide post for success, or rebelliously trying to do the opposite.

Grab a piece of paper and a pen, and write the heading, "What Success meant to my parents/guardians." Under this heading write down what you feel they viewed and imparted upon you as the meaning of Success. It doesn't matter if that's really what they viewed it as, it matters that you're defining how you interpreted it, so you can decide your own definition. Write as much as you need to get clear. Next write the heading, "What Success means to my society." Write down what you feel society deems as Success. Again, this isn't about being right or wrong, but about you getting clear about separating what you want from what you feel others want for you.

Once you've made your lists, read through what you've written and see what aspects resonate with who you want to be, and which parts do not. For those that you do not want to continue to believe in, release them by saying, "This thought no longer serves me, I choose to release it, and believe more supportive thoughts to help me achieve

my own version of Success!"

Now write the heading, "What Success means to

Me." Begin to explore this notion of Success, and what

brings you joy. What do YOU want to accomplish for

yourself? What impact can you have on this world, of any

size, that would give you great sense of achievement? Does

Success mean freedom, or wealth, or health, or happy

family, or early retirement, or all of the above? Maybe it

means bringing a brain-child into the world, or finishing a

long-standing project; whatever success means to you, in all

facets, write it all down. Get very clear on your own

definition of success. This will bring you incredible joy as you

can turn your focus in on making these important things a

reality in your life.

THANK YOU FOR THE MIRACULOUS OUTCOME!

Read through what you've written about what

Success means to you. This list should have you excited

about what is to come! It should fill you with joy, and lots of

energy; when we're in alignment with what we really want

in life, it creates a huge wave of energetic momentum!

Thinking about the journey you'll be on, and say, "Thank you

for the miraculous outcome!" for the various things on your

list that mean success to you! This will allow the Universe to help move things into alignment to make your journey creating these things a reality!

Today's To-Do List:

- First thing in the Morning do your 10 things I'm Grateful For: Make a mental or written list of 10 things you're grateful for, and for each one complete the sentence: *"Thank you, Thank you, Thank you, for _____, because _____"*
- Determine your own Success Metrics
- Get clear on how you view success
- Write out what success means to you
- Be thankful for the magnificent outcome to creating successes in your life!
- Say or think your affirmation for your Cosmic Order from Day 4: *"Thank you, thank you, thank you, for _____"*
- Remember to use your daily affirmations
- The Best Thing That Happened Today: Mentally go through your day looking for the best thing that happened to you. Once you've found the best thing, complete this sentence: *"Thank you, Thank you, Thank you, for _____ it was amazing because _____!"*

Day 18: Health

If there's one thing we take for granted above all else, it's our health; and yet, it's our health when even minutely off, that leaves us feeling more depleted, and more wanting, than anything else. Our bodies are our one and only vehicle in this life. Think to a time you had reduced health, even something minor like a cold, or allergies, or a headache; the day to day things that normally come with ease and joy suddenly feel challenging or entirely undoable.

In addition to all the things we do to keep ourselves healthy, eating good foods, sleeping enough, taking down time, and exercising our bodies, we must also be grateful for our health to continue to receive more of it. The more gratitude we have for our health and wellbeing, the more good health we will continue to receive. Any depleted health will begin to improve when we are grateful for our ideal state of being.

DIS-EASE

We've all heard of the remarkable stories of people who have healed themselves from serious, or sometimes even terminal illness, through changing the way they think.

As we learned before, we are all energy, and energy can change form. By changing our thoughts, we can change the energy in our bodies. Vitality is replenished and optimal health returns to a body when we are in a state of gratitude. When you combine gratitude with conventional healing techniques, be it modern or ancient healing practices, you're aligning your energy with that of being in optimal health.

Disease literally comes from dis-ease within the body. We've all heard that saying, "Stress causes illness," and have felt the effects of that after enduring a long period of stress and coming down with something. If you're under a great deal of stress, you're usually feeling overworked, overwhelmed, powerless, and unhappy; all easily turned around with the power of gratitude. We cannot feel unhappy and grateful at the same time, gratitude will cancel out those negative feelings.

When you reclaim your power, and remind yourself that YOU can turn around any circumstance as fast as you can think it, your stress levels will lower. Remember, any situation you're faced with, in the grand cosmic scheme of things, is very small. This will help you remember to step back and gain perspective.

Once you've taken a step back to gain perspective, ask your brain to find the best part about the situation. Your mind is like a computer, when you ask it a question, it will seek out the answer. You'll discover several aspects, of whatever is happening in your life, to be grateful for, as your mind seeks out the best. You can then ask what the easiest solution to your problem is, or how to find joy in doing the tasks you know need to be done, and see what your brain seeks out.

GRATEFUL FOR MY BODY

Our bodies are an amazing orchestra, working effortless on our part, to keep us alive. Next, I will be walking you through many of the incredible things your body does for you, without you even having to THINK about it! As I mention each function and aspect of your body, think "THANK YOU!" for that amazing vital process it's providing for you!

Think about your skeletal structure, which supports your entire body. Think about those strong bones that give your body form. Think about how your skull protects your brain, and your rib cage protects your heart and soft organs from being damaged as you go throughout your day. Think about your muscular system that allows you to move and function, from the smallest motion, to grand gestures. *Thank you bones & muscles*!

Think about your 5 senses, touch, sight, smell, hearing, and touch; these give us the ability to perceive our world! Close your eyes and try to walk around, or plug your ears and try to watch a movie, have a conversation, or listen to music, and instantly you're reminded of how important each one of these senses are to your experiences. From the pleasure of eating, to the touch of a loved one, or the scent of a flower, each of the preceptory senses enhances our lives. *Thank you eyes, ears, nose, tongue, skin, and nervous system*! *Thank you senses*!

Think about your organs, your lungs that process oxygen into your blood stream, your heart which circulates your blood and governs the function of all other organs in your body! Think about your digestive system, which absorbs nutrients, turns them into energy, replaces cells, builds muscle, and separates the waste and toxins to be expelled. Think about the chorus of them all working in unison. *Thank you organs*!

Think about your magnificent brain! No computer can match the capacity of the human brain, which is the control center for your entire body! Neurons firing speedily, as fast as we think of something, our brain jumps to action. Your thoughts, experiences, habits, memories, and all bodily processes come from your brain! *Thank you brain*!

RESTORATION

If you're currently in a state of less than optimal health; have a cold, regular headache, any kind of medical issue you're working through, arthritis, pain, stress, low energy, etc. use this restoration process along with any other medical treatment you're doing. When we feel off, it tends to be all we can think about. We focus on it, talk about it, research it; we give all our attention to being unwell. The Law of Attraction teaches us what we focus on expands, so the very LAST thing we want to do is be giving all our thoughts to the ailment.

If your ailment is specific to one body part, imagine that part, if it's effecting your entire body, picture your whole body. Imagine how it feels to be in full health, picture yourself doing the things you'd do if you weren't dealing with this ailment. Imagine how easy the day to day tasks you have become when you are in full health. Say, "Thank you, thank you, thank you, for my optimal state of health!" If you are focusing in on one specific body part, say, "Thank you, thank you, thank you _____ for functioning perfectly!" visualize yourself in peak health.

Any time your mind wanders to dwell on the negative feelings you have from your ailment, say the affirmation, "I am in perfect health!" Keep using this affirmation multiple times each day. Each time you say it, take a moment to picture yourself in optimal health. You are revitalized, healed, energized, and enjoying life to the fullest!

If you are already in excellent health, do this practice to be thankful for that state of being! You will continue to attract more great health!

Today's To-Do List:

- First thing in the Morning do your 10 things I'm Grateful For: Make a mental or written list of 10 things you're grateful for, and for each one complete the sentence: *"Thank you, Thank you, Thank you, for _____, because _____"*
- Do the Grateful for My Body Practice
- Do the Restoration Practice
- Say or think your affirmation for your Cosmic Order from Day 4: *"Thank you, thank you, thank you, for _____"*
- Remember to use your daily affirmations
- The Best Thing That Happened Today: Mentally go through your day looking for the best thing that happened to you. Once you've found the best thing, complete this sentence: *"Thank you, Thank you, Thank you, for _____ it was amazing because _____!"*

Day 19: Time

In our modern lives, if there's one phrase we hear more than any other, it's "I'm busy!" We have affirmed, reaffirmed, and ground into our minds that we are really, truly, undeniably, busy. While, yes, we're often engaged in things, we've instilled this belief so deeply within ourselves that most of us feel incredibly overwhelmed by the never-ending task list.

We live in a miraculous time; technology is an intricate part of everyday life, and it has brought the world together! We have a global online community, which is truly astounding! Any information you want to know is just one search away; we are absolutely blessed!

While technology is a true joy, helping us in so many ways, and something we cannot imagine living without, it also can be the cause of our overwhelm. We have become multi-taskers, and our attention spans have dropped significantly. According to new research, humans now have an attention span lower than that of a goldfish; and a goldfish has an attention span of just 9 seconds! *Ouch!*

Our brains are highly adaptive, and as this technological age continues to boom, we continue to learn and adapt. You pick up your phone to check your e-mail, next thing you know a text comes in and you go to see what that's all about, before you even get to the text a notification from one of your apps pops up, and then your scheduled reminder pops up, then the phone rings; it's no wonder we feel overwhelmed! Information is coming at us faster than we can process it!

The good news? This is preceptory. You're not *actually* taking on more than you can handle, it just feels that way. This isn't to say sometimes we don't bite off more than we can chew, but most of the time your feeling of being "too busy," is just a feeling. Statistics show that the average north American watches 4-5 hours of television per day, so clearly, we have time on our hands!

UNPLUG

You need time away from your tech; and yes, that may feel like a hard habit to break. Your best option is to not use your smart phone for the 1st hour you're awake in the morning, and not use it within an hour or two before going to bed. This will help you to be in the present moment more throughout your day, because you're grounding yourself in the morning by not indulging in the fast-paced technology that starts making your brain frantic.

When we pick up our phone right after we've rolled out of bed, or, worse yet, while we're still in bed, we suddenly see all these alerts, emails, texts, and notifications that make us feel like we have a monumental task to get through that day. We feel defeated before the day has even started. When you wake up and give yourself time to ease into your day, to take stock, plan out your day, and get perspective on what's important that day, you've got both hands on the wheel. When you then look at your phone, all those notification don't seem so overwhelming, because you already know what your day is about to look like, and you can quickly plow through checking all of those notifications. The Magic Morning is a great way for you to have this time to yourself in the morning without your tech, to be in the present moment.

Setting your smart phone down at night, at least for the hour before bed, helps your brain to slow down. This will help you to relax, and therefore, give you a better night's rest. When we're well rested our minds are sharper, again giving you that sense of control over your life. You're in the driver's seat, so put both hands on the wheel!

TIP: Put your phone on airplane mode for the first hour of the morning and the last hour of the evening, or completely turn your phone off so you're not tempted to look at it!

GET ORGANIZED

We're very quick to adapt to new routines, so adapting new habits around your tech and your daily tasks will leave you feeling in control and liberated! At the beginning of each day take 3-5 minutes to plan out the things you need and want to do that day with pen and paper. If you normally use a to-do list app, you can input it into your phone while it's on airplane mode BUT you do not have permission to click on anything else but this app, and must put the phone away immediately afterwards. You need that hour of tech free time in the morning for you.

Your clear daily to-do list is going to help you see just how much you can accomplish and that it doesn't take as much time as you feel when you go in without a plan. The other thing we need to organize is our use of time on our smart phones and computers. When you start a task, don't let yourself go and do another task before completing the first one. For example, if you're using your smart phone to check and reply to e-mail, you do not have permission to go and check your text messages until you've completed your e-mails tasks. This will help improve your concentration, and give you a greater sense of accomplishment. When we flip from one task to the next without finishing them, we feel like we're drowning in all the things we need to do. But when you do a task and complete it, you check it off the list, and are able to move onto the next one, knowing you're making headway.

SELF-TALK

Quite possibly the most challenging part of this exercise will be changing your self-talk about how busy you are. It is time to ditch, "I'm busy," and "I'm too busy," from your mental and verbal vocabulary. As long as you continue to say and think that you're "too busy," The Universe is going to keep on throwing things at you to keep you busy. The Universe will give you everything you focus on, so it's time to attract more time!

Your new mantra is, "I have plenty of time!" say it often out loud, and in your head. You're de-weeding your belief garden of "I'm too busy," and planting the need seed of, "I have plenty of time!" which means you need to nurture that seed! Help that thought grow and take root in your mind by giving in lots of attention!

We're used to using "I'm too busy," as an excuse when we don't want to do something we've been invited to. We also often say, "I've been busy," when someone asks us, "How have you been lately?" It's become a lazy response, and because what we say we believe, we need to cut that habit and usage out too. If you're doing something else, or have other plans, say so! If someone asks how you've been as of late, share what you've been up to! These will make for much more interesting conversations and get you out of believing that you're so dang busy!

BREATHE

If you're in the midst of overwhelm, one of the simplest and most helpful things we can do to stop it, is breathe. Focused, intentional breathing, can calm the nervous system, and help us to get back into the moment. Place your hand on your lower abdominal and breathe in through your nose, feeling your belly rise, on a slow 8 count, then hold your breath for a slow 10 count, and exhales through your mouth for a slow 8 count, feeling your belly

release. Do this 2-3 times in a row, or as many times as you

wish, and you will feel a sense of calm and peace. It can also

help to imagine you are breathing in a calm loving energy,

and exhaling stress and anxiety.

Today's To-Do List:

- First thing in the Morning do your 10 things I'm Grateful For: Make a mental or written list of 10 things you're grateful for, and for each one complete the sentence: *"Thank you, Thank you, Thank you, for _____, because _____"*
- Commit to UNPLUG
- Get Organized with a daily to-do list and with how you handle your tech tasks!
- Adopt the mantra, "I have plenty of time!"
- Use the breathing technique on 3 separate occasions today
- Say or think your affirmation for your Cosmic Order from Day 4: *"Thank you, thank you, thank you, for _____ "*
- Remember to use your daily affirmations
- The Best Thing That Happened Today: Mentally go through your day looking for the best thing that happened to you. Once you've found the best thing, complete this sentence: *"Thank you, Thank you, Thank you, for _____ it was amazing because _____!"*

Day 20: Abundance

Living in abundance is all about leading a rich fulfilling life in all areas. It is about balance, and it is about not holding back; releasing fear and embracing new experiences and opportunities. Throughout this book you've learned that your thoughts create your reality, and therefore, you know abundance in all areas of your life is but a shift in thought patterns away.

Think to a time where you were around someone inspirational, who left you feeling like you could do, be, or accomplish anything. These people acted in spite of fear, naysayers, doubters, ridiculers, and made their mark in the world, in a way that is a marvel to all around them. When we look at those who inspire us, we often tend to think how lucky they are, and forget to acknowledge the struggles they endured to create their achievements. Many failures paved their path to success, many obstacles, and many moments of fighting the urge to quit. Living large isn't about luck, it's about belief, unshakable faith, and vision. When you set out to live big you'll have your share of tests, but, you will also have the Universe to back you up! Once you're in motion, committed, and believing, the Universe will move things into place to support you in such incredible symphony that you'd think it was magic!

Living small, hiding your natural talents from the world, it serves no one and diminishes us all; but when you shine your light, live big, and share your natural gifts with the world, we all benefit. When you step up to live big, your presence becomes an inspiration to all of those in your presence. You inspire others to become their best self, to push past their fears, and to share their incredible gifts with the world. This ripple effect can completely change the world at large.

LIVE LARGE

Look at your Top 10 Manifestation List, and ask yourself, "Am I playing big or choosing things that feel 'safe'?" Don't judge what you want, we all want different things out of life; the key is that your list comes from your heart and isn't being limited by fear, or past unsupportive belief systems. People often fear being viewed as greedy, or what people will think of them if they go all-out after our dreams. Remember to *beware of the crabs* when these thoughts come up; follow your own path. And what if we fail? Those fearful thoughts creep up and you need to tell yourself, "if I don't try I have already failed." If need be, re-write your list.

Living large is a life of personal growth, triumph, and learning. It will help you to face your fears, and push through them, as your goals become more important than all the "What ifs?" your brain can muster. Trying and failing helps us learn, and we come to terms with failure not being bad, and instead a tool to help us grow. We learn the truth: we only truly fail if we give up!

When you step up to the plate, and say "I'm going all in!" the Universe will have your back. You will have all the resources available to you; just keep focused on the goal and flex that faith muscle. You're on the road to success.

INVITE THE UNIVERSE TO GET INVOLVED

The Universe is always there for you, 24/7, at the speed of thought. The more you remember to rely on the Universe, incorporating daily gratitude. as well as focusing on what you want instead of what you don't want, the more the Universe can support you on your journey. The Universe can also bring abundance your way, in many forms, upon request! Tell the Universe you are ready to receive!

"Universe, I am ready and willing to receive all of your blessings! Thank you!"

This simple communication shows gratitude for the abundance the Universe will provide, and states your intention and desire. Many people are poor receivers. Giving and receiving are forms of energy, two sides of the same coin. Whoever started the saying, "it's better to give than to receive," was full of baloney! Is night better than day? Is hot better than cold? They're both equally important.

Have you ever giving someone a gift and they were awkward or ungrateful for it? How did that make you feel? Pretty awful! Your flowing energy to them was abruptly halted by their inability to receive. On the other hand, think to a time when you gave someone a gift that they were so happy to receive, their joy became your joy! Get good at receiving! You enjoying, and being grateful for, what you get will ensure more of the good keep flowing to you!

Today's To-Do List:

- First thing in the Morning do your 10 things I'm Grateful For: Make a mental or written list of 10 things you're grateful for, and for each one complete the sentence: *"Thank you, Thank you, Thank you, for _____, because _____"*

- Commit to UNPLUG

- Review your Top 10 manifestation list, and, if need be, re-write it to support living large

- Invite the Universe to Get Involved

- Say or think your affirmation for your Cosmic Order from Day 4: *"Thank you, thank you, thank you, for _____"*

- Remember to use your daily affirmations

- The Best Thing That Happened Today: Mentally go through your day looking for the best thing that happened to you. Once you've found the best thing, complete this sentence: *"Thank you, Thank you, Thank you, for _____ it was amazing because _____!"*

Day 21: Living with Daily Gratitude

We are always manifesting, so the integration of purposeful daily manifesting, through gratitude, is the key to manifesting your life on purpose. When we're not consciously manifesting, we're unconsciously manifesting; our minds wander, we dwell on what's happening instead of the future we want to create, and we get stuck in a feedback loop. Through daily practice, you'll train your brain to always seek out the good, to focus on what you want instead of what you don't want, and the results will show up in your life!

After these 3 weeks of back to back practices, if you did them without days off in between, you should already be noticing a major shift in your mindset.   If you did miss days and spread this out longer you'll still notice a difference, however I would recommend going back to day 1 and committing to all 21 days in a row to get these habits down pat! The cumulative act of purposeful thought, day after day, helps you to become much more aware of your thoughts, and old beliefs when they crop up, allowing you to able to quickly shift your thoughts any time negativity crops back up.

When you make gratitude part of your daily life, you will be attracting abundance to you effortlessly. A grateful heart means you're choosing to focus on the good, you're aligning your energy with the things you're grateful for, whether it's something you already have or something you'd like to have, when you're grateful for it the Universe brings it, or more of it, to you! This is the main reason we have used the Day 1 Practice each and every day throughout this book! You're now automatically choosing to look for the good in every situation!

CREATING YOUR DAILY PRACTICE

Creating a daily practice is pure joy! You have been experiencing many different ways to practice the Law of Attraction through these 3 weeks, so you have an array of options to choose from! Grab a piece of paper and a pen and write down your favorite practices from these past 3 weeks. Follow your intuition: what felt right? What was fun? What did you want to do again? Some practices, like making a vision board, you might not necessarily want to do daily, but could be a fun monthly practice if it really helped you feel excited to see all of your desires in image form! Maybe you loved the magic morning, or have a specific area of your life you want to work on, like your love life, career, or finances; you can hone in on what you want to focus on!

You can piece-meal together anything you like to form your own practice that works for you! There is no wrong way to do this. If following these daily practices as they've been laid out helped you feel a great sense of structure and balance, you can keep repeating it as often as you wish!

Let's say you wrote this down as your list:

Favorite Practices:

Morning Gratitude's

Evening best thing that happened today

Money

Career

Meditation

Placing my Cosmic order

So, with this list, you might decide to do your 10 things I'm grateful for in the morning followed by the Affirmations, "I am a money magnet!" and, "Opportunities come to me effortlessly!". Following that you might decide to do one of the activities from the Money day exercises, such as visualizing using the Nature Abhors a Vacuum practice. Next, you'd place your Cosmic Order. At night you'd sit in quiet meditation for the length of your choosing, followed by doing The Best Thing that Happened to me Today gratitude practice before going to sleep. This is just one example of how you might formulate your daily practice!

Follow your heart and pick the practices that bring you the most joy. Schedule in the time to do the practices as is needed; and remember you can be grateful throughout your day without having to stop what you're doing too! The more you practice, the more an integral part of your life purposeful manifesting and gratitude will become!

Take a look over your list and then track back through our lessons to pick out your favorite activities and affirmations, and put together your practice. You can try it out, change what doesn't feel right, or continuously mix it up! The choice is yours; the key is that whatever you do, do something daily to keep your manifesting skills sharp!

REMEMBER TO SURRENDER

Throughout your journey, remember to trust the Universe. Keep in mind always that we have limited perspective, and the Universe can see everything, and guide us to better outcomes than we can even imagine IF we allow it. As you work to manifest your dreams, be open to alternatives that come your way. Use, "...this or something better!" on your manifesting requests to give the Universe room to work! Do not get so dead set on any one thing that you block off possible better options. Sometimes the Universe can see that the business you want that loan for is going to tank for any number of unforeseen factors; or sometimes we want something SO bad, so desperately, that we end up repelling it because we don't have faith that it will come. Want what you want, visualize it, be grateful for it, but don't force it. Release it to the Universe and know that it will bring you what your heart desires... or something even better!

Today's To-Do List:

- First thing in the Morning do your 10 things I'm Grateful For: Make a mental or written list of 10 things you're grateful for, and for each one complete the sentence: *"Thank you, Thank you, Thank you, for* _____*, because* _____ *"*
- Create your Daily Law of Attraction Practice to use here on out!
- Say or think your affirmation for your Cosmic Order from Day 4: *"Thank you, thank you, thank you, for* _____ *"*
- Remember to use your daily affirmations
- The Best Thing That Happened Today: Mentally go through your day looking for the best thing that happened to you. Once you've found the best thing, complete this sentence: *"Thank you, Thank you, Thank you, for* _____ *it was amazing because* _____ *!"*

Thank You for Joining me on this Journey!

Love & Light,

Amanda Rose

Author's Other Works

- Manifesting Your Best Life

- Fire Fury Freedom

- Fire Fury Frontier

- The Impending End

- A Strange Dream

Manifesting Your Best Life:

How to Stop Wishing for Change and Start Living Your Best Life

AMANDA ROSE

MANIFESTING YOUR BEST LIFE

How to Stop Wishing for Change and Start Living Your Best Life

Manifesting Your Best Life Book Description:

Stop dreaming about a better life and start living it!

Manifesting You Best Life is going to show you that "Living Your Best Life" isn't just some cute meme on social media – it can be your way of life! The 21 nugget-of-wisdom chapters in this self-help book are for people who want to start living their best life, but don't know where to begin. It will give you the skills to take you from dreaming about your best life, to making it your reality!

You will learn:
•How to Identify what living your best life really means to you.
•The steps needed to stop wishing and start living your best life.
•How to use the Law of Attraction to support your efforts.
•Successful habits that will change your life.
•And how to create the life you've always wanted... And start living it NOW!

By the end of Manifesting Your Best Life, you will have a clear picture of what your dream life looks like, how to get there, and the tools and skills to make it into your reality!
Are you ready to begin?

Fire Fury Freedom

"A veritable saga of a dystopian novel by an author with a genuine flair for detailed originality, and narrative driven storytelling, "Fire Fury Freedom" by Amanda Rose is an extraordinary and truly memorable read from cover to cover." -*Midwest Book Review*

Prequel to the Fire Fury Frontier Series

Fire Fury Freedom Book Description:

A dying planet on the verge of collapse…. tormented pasts that haunt the present… an ancient hidden magick…

The C.D.F.P. mega-corporation rules all, with unchecked power, and dark secrets…

The planet is dying, and they are the last hope to save it… Mack, an ex-soldier of the C.D.F.P. military division, and his mercenaries, standalone against the C.D.F.P. (AKA the Company), in the fight for humanities survival. Left unchallenged, the company has ruled over the East Green Continent with an iron fist for decades. The pollution they've caused has devastated the planet, destroying the ozone, and killing off plant and animal life.

Outside of domed cities the air is thin, and the sun scorches all; it's a veritable wasteland. In the past two decades the planet has reached entirely new levels of decay. Extreme weather patterns, and massive quakes, ravage the land.

Time is running out…

Mack and his mercenary troupe set out on a quest to stop the C.D.F.P. once and for all, and the planet will test them to their limits… But are they ready for the horrors they'll uncover? Can they alone stand up against the all-powerful C.D.F.P.?

Fire Fury Frontier

Fire Fury Frontier Book Description:

One ship, one last chance to survive...

Humanity's home world has been destroyed from extensive global warming. For over two hundred years the last remaining humans have lived in space aboard a single massive ship, the Saisei. After generations in space, living aboard a ship is all anyone has ever known.

But space is an inhospitable home.

The ship is old and damaged, rations are low, and a planet fit for colonization has never been found.

In the vast expanse of space, as the Saisei makes way to resupply their ship, they stumble upon a discovery that will change the course of human history forever.

The Impending End

The Impending End Book Description:

It's 2005. Ayla Jefferson is 17, incredibly intelligent, sensitive, imaginative, and thoughtful. She's also contemplating suicide...

After a life long battle with mental illness plaguing her every move, Ayla is ready for death. Eerily calm, she says her goodbyes, and sets out to commit her final act.

But despite her stubborn conviction, life isn't as easy to let go of as she expected. Her hyper-imagination blurs reality and she finds herself getting lost in gripping memories. Mentally disengaged, Ayla's experiences are surreal, and discerning fact from fiction becomes harder and harder.

As the life she's so eager to leave behind begs to hold on, will she be able to leave it all behind?

A Strange Dream

Anthology of Short Stories and Poetry

A Strange Dream Book Description:

Death, Depression, Insomnia, Prostitution, Eating Disorders, Abortion, Convicts, Insanity, and Marital issues... This anthology of short stories and poetry explores the dark reaches of the mind and mental health issues.

The 9 short stories, including award winning EGGS and OUTSIDER, as well as runner up in the Canadian Writer's Guild Short Prose competition, DROWNING IN SILENCE, and 9 poems, take us on a journey from the surreal to the mundane. From day-to-day life to fantasy, the characters and situations explore many walks of life.